THE HUGUENOTS

THE HUGUENOTS

By

A. J. GRANT

ARCHON BOOKS
1969

FIRST PUBLISHED 1934
REPRINTED 1969 WITH PERMISSION
IN AN UNALTERED AND UNABRIDGED EDITION

SBN: 208 00745 8
LIBRARY OF CONGRESS CATALOG CARD NUMBER: 69-11552
PRINTED IN THE UNITED STATES OF AMERICA

SHOE STRING PRESS

4.20

CONTENTS

5

46637

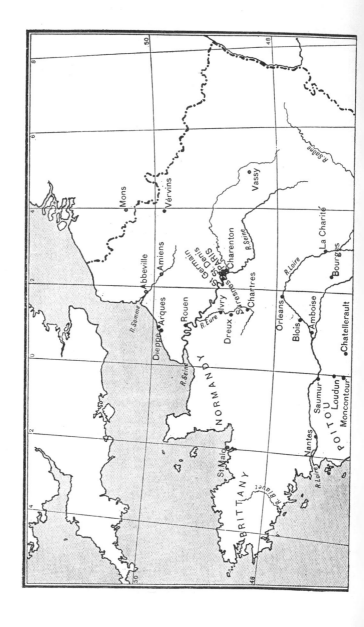

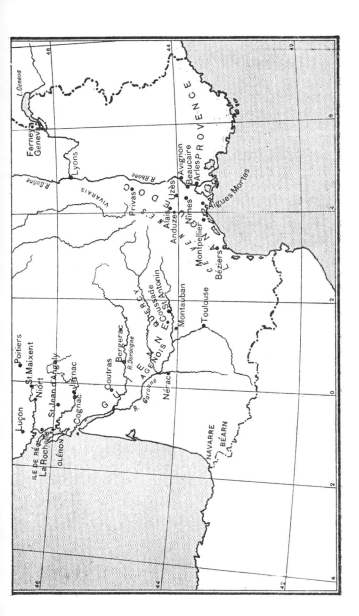

PREFACE

THE story that I have had to tell is a long one and in order to enclose it within the limits assigned by the Home University Library I have had to choose certain parts of it for fuller treatment than others. I have passed as rapidly as possible over the religious wars of the sixteenth century, though that has made it necessary to pay scant attention to such interesting figures as Coligny and Catherine de Médicis and Henry of Navarre. I have given more attention and a fuller treatment to the seventeenth and eighteenth centuries ; to the Revocation of the Edict and to the heroic recovery of the Huguenots from the catastrophe that had befallen them. With the concurrence of the Editor I have added a slight chapter on French Protestantism since the Great Revolution.

I may add that I have written on the history of the Huguenots in the sixteenth century at some length in *A History of Europe, 1494–1610*, published by Messrs. Methuen.

CHAPTER I

FRANCE had her full share in the religious un-settlement of the sixteenth century. All the features that characterized the religious life of western Europe were to be found there ; a Church wealthy and powerful, provoking opposition and criticism by its wealth and its influence on government ; a vast network of monastic establishments, where in buildings of surpassing beauty many different types of religious life were practised, where by the side of austere devotion to the ideals of Saint Benedict and Saint Bernard were to be found the greatest laxity of life and aims that were purely secular ; parish priests, poor, laborious and devoted, and also very many who in character, education and aims were hardly to be distinguished from the peasants among whom they lived ; an almost universal conventional acceptance of the doctrines and practices of the Roman Catholic Church, with here and there in monastery or cathedral close or parish priest's home a wonderful readiness to criticize and discuss and reject. Such features were common to France with England, Germany, Italy, the Netherlands, and even Spain

It is more important to notice certain features which are more peculiar to France. There was first the theory and sentiment of Gallicanism, which colours and influences all French history during the sixteenth century to an extent much greater than is usually realized by English observers. In the midst of the Religious Wars Cardinal Guise, whose devotion to Rome was above question, declared that he no more doubted the principles of Gallicanism than the central doctrines of Christianity. And yet it is difficult to define Gallicanism. It was French nationalism expressed in terms of religion ; it was the view that France must be mistress in her own house in matters religious as well as in politics. Something of the sort was strong in most countries of Europe ; it was a feeling of this kind which contributed most powerfully to the English breach with Rome in the reign of Henry VIII ; it is implied in Luther's appeals to German national sentiment. But the desire for national independence in matters of religion had gained a more complete triumph in France than elsewhere before the Reformation ; and though this triumph is in harmony with one of the strongest elements in Protestantism the fact that it had come without schism made schism less attractive. From 1438 (the Pragmatic Sanction of Bourges) the control of the Church in France had been in the hands of French churchmen, who appointed Archbishops, Bishops, and Abbots and limited carefully the flow of payments to Rome. That settlement, however, had given the Church in

France a large measure of independence of the French Kings as well as of the Roman Pope ; and, when the chance came, it was modified in the interests of the royal power. In 1515 King Francis I found himself in a position to dictate his will to the powers of Italy, including the papacy itself ; for the battle of Marignano had made him for the moment the one military power in Europe. His negotiations with Pope Leo X led to the signing of the Concordat of Bologna. To the Pope were given increased revenues from the French Church, but the real control of that Church was transferred from the churchmen themselves to the monarchy. Henceforth the Kings appointed the great ecclesiastics and were thus able, like the Kings of England later, to " tune the pulpits." They also had a very large power over the disposal of Church funds and used them unscrupulously for their own personal and political ends. Thus on the eve of the Reformation the Church in France was to a very large extent a national and royal Church. The connexion with Rome was not of course broken nor even seriously threatened ; there was no breach in doctrine and no very wide divergence in religious forms ; the Kings of France were officially " most Christian." The significance of the Concordat of Bologna for the coming age is that the Church in France was henceforward no longer a rival but an ally and almost a servant of the Kings of France. Nearly everywhere in Europe where Protestantism was victorious it owed much of its triumph to an alliance with nationalism.

But of such alliance there was no likelihood in France, for the wealth and the influence of the Roman Church were already at the disposal of the Crown.

Independent thought and propaganda then in matters of religion encountered the opposition of Crown as well as Church in France. This opposition acted mainly through two agencies which it is important to understand. These were the Parlements of France (and especially the Parlement of Paris) and the Sorbonne. The Parlements were the highest legal corporations of France, and the Parlement of Paris was the most important of them, because it functioned over the widest area and was in immediate contact with the King and his Court. The history of the monarchy of France was closely connected with that of this Parlement. By its means the Kings had broken down the independence of the nobles and had tamed the pretensions of the ecclesiastics of France. It was full of pride and self-confidence and was beginning to claim powers that would make it a rival instead of a servant of the monarchy. It was specially jealous of the authority of ecclesiastics. Some of its members were attracted by the new religious ideas, but for the most part the orthodoxy of the Parlement was beyond suspicion. It was ready to suppress heresy, but it insisted that the suppression must be in its own hands. The Inquisition, with its independent tribunals and procedure, was never admitted into France. The Parlement hunted and burnt heretics itself and humanity gained little by the substitution of a secular for an ecclesiastical tribunal.

The other institution that has been mentioned —the Sorbonne—represented the great University of Paris, the most influential of the Universities of Europe during the Middle Ages. It was divided into four Faculties—Arts, Theology, Law and Medicine. The Sorbonne was simply the theological Faculty of the University of Paris. It had no judicial powers, but its authority in all matters that concerned " heresy " was naturally great. It was strongly Gallican in spirit and extremely jealous of papal interference in France ; but its members were for the most part thoroughly hostile to the new thought that was spreading through Europe. Scholasticism in its bad sense—the arid and profitless worship of tradition, the pedantic insistence on definitions, the enthusiasm for hair splitting —found one of its chief supports in the Sorbonne.

France was in the forefront of the intellectual movement of Europe and of all those tendencies that are vaguely summed up as the Renaissance, and unorthodox religious speculation had made early appearance on her soil. As soon as the movement of Luther was known in France his opinions were submitted to the Sorbonne. They declared them a dangerous heresy, menacing alike to Church and society, and asked for their extirpation " by fire rather than by reason." But the movement continued and spread. Many ecclesiastics were attracted by different sides of the new opinions. There was especially an interesting movement of

Reform within the bounds of the Roman and
Catholic Church at Meaux where Briçonnet was
Bishop. But the movement died away or was
crushed out; we cannot follow its interesting
history. Francis I was reckoned to be open to
new ideas and has the name of " the King of the
Renaissance." He was for political reasons in
alliance with the German Protestants, but at the
end of his reign he became thoroughly alarmed
at the spread of the new ideas and struck at their
supporters with pitiless severity. His successor,
Henry II, was even more determined to repress
by the severest punishments all variations from
established orthodoxy.

All types of religious heresy in France were at
first labelled " Lutheranism "; but soon her
rulers became aware of a movement which had
its origin in France itself, whose books were written
in French, whose founder and lifelong leader was
himself a Frenchman. It is to the growth and history of this movement—the contribution of France
to Protestantism—that this little book is devoted.

John Calvin was born at Noyon, in Picardy, in
1509. He was thus Luther's junior by more than
a quarter of a century and this fact is of decisive
importance for the man and his movement. When
Calvin became the leading figure of the Protestant
world the early hopes of an easy and complete
victory for the new ideas had passed away. It
was clear that the world was not going to rally to
the " Evangel " with spontaneous enthusiasm.
The Roman Church was entrenched within a

magnificent organization whose defects and decay could easily be remedied ; it was defended by vested interests of power and wealth. Above all it was deeply rooted in the traditions, the affections, and the beliefs of a large part of the population of Europe. It was natural that the Protestant leaders should in the bitterness of the struggle charge those who would not join them, or who having joined them fell away from them, with cowardice and self-interest. But history ought not to fall into the mistake. There was in Europe in the sixteenth century a clash of power and economic interests and this had a great influence on the religious conflict. But there was also a struggle of a genuinely religious character ; ideals were pitted against ideals, faith against faith ; love and devotion were to be found on either side. Thus when Calvin became the leader of the Protestant movement it had clearly to fight hard for victory and even for survival. What was wanted was discipline, definition of aim and programme, organization. And all these Calvin gave with a success which made him second only to Luther in his influence on the Protestant world, and in some ways his influence was even greater than Luther's.

He was designed by his father for the priesthood and after the fashion of the age was provided even as a child with benefices in the Church. He went to the University of Paris to study theology. But either he or his father was dissatisfied with a clerical career. Calvin determined to study law and moved in 1527 to Orleans where the university was famous for its legal studies. In 1531 he was at Bourges University. He returned to Paris, and in 1532 published a commentary on Seneca's treatise on Mercy. The only importance of this book is that it may remind us that Calvin was an excellent classical scholar. But about this time a new force had mastered him and his life had taken its master bias. He had been converted. Of the time when it occurred and of the agencies by which it was brought about we know little : but its intensity and sincerity are written broadly across the history of Europe for the rest of the century and far beyond that. He was no religious leader as yet and was not called on to face the dangers which menaced Protestants in France. In the German towns of the Rhine he would find a freer atmosphere and many of his own country-men. He went to Basel and there in 1536 he published the *Institutes of the Christian Religion*. 1536 is the decisive date of his career. He passed through Geneva intending to stay there only for a day. Geneva was already Protestant of the free type which prevailed in Protestant Switzerland. The leading Protestant Minister was Farel, a Frenchman like Calvin. He was struggling against much opposition and wanted help. He entreated Calvin to stay and help him ; and with some difficulty he prevailed. Two years later the opposition gathered strength and Calvin was driven from Geneva. He withdrew willingly from what he had been feeling to be a great burden. He lived in exile most of three years and most of the time

in Strasburg.   He worked ; he wrote ; he married ;
he was still a prominent figure among those who
had broken from the Roman communion.   He
spoke of his life at Geneva with horror.   But
Geneva had not been peaceful in his absence.
Dangers accumulated outside and inside of the
little city.   There is some resemblance to the victory of Fascism in Italy or to that of Hitlerism in
Germany in the return of Calvin to Geneva.   Not
liberty but a single definite aim consistently and
relentlessly pursued seemed necessary to give
solidity to the state and victory over her enemies.
So Calvin was invited back again.   With some
hesitation he accepted the invitation and it
was from Geneva that his influence streamed
on to Europe until the day of his death in
1564.

French Protestantism is Calvinism ; " the Huguenots " was the nickname given to those in France
who adopted his doctrine and scheme of life.   It
is necessary therefore to understand his work in
Geneva before we turn to trace the fortunes of the
Huguenots in France.

The Genevan system assumed that all citizens
were members of the Evangelical Church.   There
was not therefore any of the conflict between Church
and state, which is so important a feature of nearly
all other European States.   There was of course
the machinery of a secular state at Geneva—two
councils and a General Assembly—but with these
we have no concern.   It is the religious life which
alone interests us.

17

At the back of all lies the theology of Calvin, summed up in the successive editions of the *Institutes of the Christian Religion*. All rested on the authority of the scriptures. " I have not to my knowledge," he wrote, " corrupted or twisted a single passage of the Scriptures." And from this source he had derived without any doubt or question the doctrine of predestination in its completest form. Luther indeed held the same doctrine and declared that he found it in Saint Augustine, but it is from the writings of Calvin that the Protestant world derived it in its most absolute form. One may say that it is the whole of Calvin's theology; and yet he summarizes it in a few sentences. Thus at the end of Book III, chapter 21, he writes :

" In conformity to the clear teaching of scripture we assert that by an eternal and immutable counsel God hath once for all determined both whom he would admit to salvation and whom he would condemn to destruction. We affirm that this counsel, as far as concerns the elect, is founded on his gratuitous mercy, totally irrespective of human merit ; but that to those whom he devotes to condemnation the gate of life is closed by a just and irreprehensible but incomprehensible judgment." The Huguenots of France and the Puritans of the seventeenth century are not to be understood unless we remember always that they faced life with the temper that this doctrine gave them. They were the chosen soldiers of God in a war where victory was certain.

The government of the Church was vested in a consistory, consisting of six ministers and twelve laymen. It was the business of the consistory to enforce the discipline which was the most striking feature of the Church in Geneva. It is noteworthy that this important body contained a majority of laymen. And throughout the Genevan system as established by Calvin it is to be noted how great were the duties allotted to laymen. The prominent co-operation of laymen in the life of the Church was indeed one of the foremost and most important marks of Calvinism, and it had consequences, political and social as well as religious. But it must always be remembered that it was assumed that these laymen would be adherents of the Calvinist Church. For Geneva was to be a theocracy in the strictest sense.

Life at Geneva was to be regulated by the Church in every important detail. When Calvin returned to Geneva after his exile he laid it down as one of his prime conditions " that no church could exist unless a fixed rule of life in accordance with the Word of God were laid down," and in the preamble to the rules of the nascent Church it was written " that it would be well to lay down a mode of life for every one." The monasteries were destroyed and the monastic rule denounced ; but a rule in some ways stricter than that of the monasteries was introduced, not only for those who chose it of their free will but for all the inhabitants of Geneva. English, Scotch, and American Puritanism was born in Geneva. The details of the lives of men

and women were regulated; their dress, their
meals, their songs, their presents. Indiscipline
was punished with Church censures and sometimes
with severe penalties. The twentieth century finds
all this an intolerable tyranny. To many in the
sixteenth it was welcomed as raising life to a higher
plane. To the Scotchman Knox it seemed the
greatest thing in Europe. It was certainly a discipline of first-rate importance in the great religious
contest which had to be waged for the next century
and a half.

We have no space for any further examination
of the Genevan Utopia. But we must note that
Calvin took on the question of the Eucharist a
view which separated him from all other Protestant
bodies as well as from the Roman Church. He
insisted in his catechism on its importance and
the need of more frequent communion than had
been usual; he says it is a sacrament which ex-
hibits the " secret union of Christ with the faithful,
which is incomprehensible by nature," and that
" our souls are fed by the flesh and blood of Christ
just as our corporeal life is preserved and sustained
by bread and wine." His doctrine was thus as far
removed from the commemorative ceremony of
Zwingli as it was from the consubstantiation of
Luther. Neither he nor his immediate followers
would abate a jot of what he had written in the
fourth Book of the *Institutes*.

Thus at Geneva a Frenchman was building up
a Protestant Faith and Church with classical
definiteness and uniformity and was training a

force with the temper of steel to defend it. We must now turn away from Geneva and see how this movement came or came back to France and what its fortunes were there.

I am attempting in this little book to sketch the fortunes of the Protestants of France, and must assume some knowledge of the general course of French history. But it will be well to mark some of the chief turning-points. The monarchy was strong and popular ; it had delivered France from the agony of the English wars and shared in the general movement which promoted strong monarchies throughout western Europe. King Charles VIII in 1494 had opened the long series of wars for the possession of Italy, which were a master passion with the French Kings for at least half a century. Their great opponent was the power of Spain, which may almost be identified with the House of Hapsburg which held the imperial throne and ruled in the " Austrian " lands. In the Italian wars the French Kings had gained some splendid triumphs, but had in the end failed to make good their foothold in Italy. These wars have a close relation to the religious movement because the French Kings, in order to create diffi-culties for the Austro-Spanish power north of the Alps, had allied themselves with the Protestants of Germany ; and there can be no doubt that their alliance saved the followers of Luther from imminent risk of destruction. This alliance of King Francis I with Protestant Germany and his interest in the art of the Renaissance made some French reformers entertain great hopes of him, and Calvin had dedicated his *Christian Institutes* to him, protesting against the view that his followers desired " to subvert all order and governments " and desiring " to prepare your mind to attend to the pleading of our cause." But as we have seen, the King's ears were quite deaf to his pleading. Hard blows fell on the Protestants and Crespin's martyrology has many stories to tell of suffering and heroism during these years. Nor was the lot of religious dissidents improved when Henry II came to the throne in 1547. His foreign policy showed the same anti-Spanish and pro-Protestant trend, but at home he was determined to maintain religious uniformity and communion with Rome.

A new era opened when a chance stroke in a tournament killed Henry II in 1559 and made his son Francis II King of France. The new King was a weak, sickly boy and ruled only in name. For nearly twenty years the most important figure and influence in France was the Queen Mother, the notorious Catherine de Médicis. Her character and career have been so obscured by religious and political animosity, and drama and romance have so powerfully contributed to popularize the impression thus created, that it is difficult even to attempt to see her as she was. If we could take away from her record one terrible crime—the massacre of Saint Bartholomew's Day—she would without doubt be recognized as the most persistent supporter of a policy of balance and mutual toleration in the religious conflicts of the time. But that crime cannot be taken away nor forgotten. It was indeed no part of a deliberate plan and may almost be called accidental. But that she could be driven into it by whatever motives—policy or fear or ambition—shows how far she was from true statesmanship. She was a characteristic Italian woman of the century, interested in art and thought, enjoying intensely the good things of life—food and drink and social life—passionately fond of power, from which she had been kept aloof during the life of her husband, an adherent of the Roman and Catholic Church but entirely without religious passion or sincerity of belief. She desired personal power and in pursuit of this end she modified her policy from day to day. That policy was opportunist and personal and without long views. But one of her first acts was to make the wise and humane L'Hôpital Chancellor of France and to try to find a way out of the impending religious war by means of a measure of toleration. When at the end of the century toleration at last triumphed in the Edict of Nantes, and gave France a century of domestic peace and progress, it was Catherine who had shown the way to Henry of Navarre.

The Queen Mother and her young son had grave tasks to face both at home and abroad. It is only of the domestic problem that we must speak and only of that part of it which sprang from religious differences. The persecutions of the last two reigns had not destroyed Protestantism. The new doctrine from Geneva had penetrated the country by various channels. Colporteurs carried books and pamphlets. Preachers risked their lives—and sometimes paid the forfeit—to minister to congregations of the faithful. The movement spread apace. Many no doubt were attracted by certain sides of the new thought without wishing to break away from the Roman communion ; but groups of real adherents formed themselves, drawn from most of the social classes of France ; though the peasantry do not seem to have been drawn to the new faith, except where as in the Vaudois there was a traditional opposition to the Roman Church. There were monks and priests among the Huguenots—we will speak of them by this name henceforward though it was not yet in common use—though there was nothing like that stampede of the clergy into the ranks of the new Church which is so noticeable in Germany. A strongly marked characteristic of the Protestant movement in France is the large adhesion of noblemen to its ranks. The whole history of the Huguenots is coloured by this fact, which is difficult to explain. But the nobles of France had been the most dangerous rivals of the monarchy ; and, though they had been worsted, they did not yet accept their defeat, and were glad to carry on their opposition to the Crown under the cloak of religion and with the help of religious organizations. But though selfish motives may without cynicism be conjectured in many of them, some of the titled Huguenots—such as the Queen of Navarre, Coligny and du Plessis-Mornay—were among the most

24

sincere and passionate supporters of the new faith. It will be well before we plunge into the confusion of the religious wars to gain some acquaintance with the leading Huguenots of France about the year 1558.

We cannot number the Huguenots at the accession of Francis II, nor can we enter into their gatherings and see them worshipping after the fashion that had been adopted in Geneva. But the real secret of the strength of the movement lay there. There is a tendency in some of the histories of the time to lay too much stress on the aristocratic leaders and the political reactions of the Reform movement in France. But the real driving-power came from the large body of faithful people, for whom the teaching of Calvin had given a new meaning to life and who embraced with enthusiasm its hopes and discipline and mode of life. Before a century had passed the aristocratic leaders fell away, and in a century and a half the political aspirations of the Huguenots had led to complete disaster ; but the movement survived contempt and cruel persecution, supported by the faith and patience of the common man.

Theodore de Beza (or Bèze in the French form) was much the most prominent of the French ministers of religion. His career had run parallel with that of Calvin. He had frequented the Universities of Paris and Bourges, had abjured Catholicism and had withdrawn first into Germany and then to Geneva. He was at first a Lutheran, but later had adopted with enthusiasm the views of Calvin. As the movement spread in France he returned thither and devoted his tongue and his pen—both of them extremely active—to the propaganda of his faith and the defence of his co-religionaries. He was the perfect type of Calvinist minister and is to be found at the very centre of the whole movement in France down to his death in 1605. He has many points of resemblance with John Knox, but never dominated the political situation as Knox did.

Three brothers of the noble house of Montmorency played a large part in the councils and policy of the Huguenots ; François d'Andelot : Odet, Cardinal de Chatillon and Bishop of Beauvais : and most important of all Gaspard de Coligny, Admiral of France. They were members of one of the two greatest families in France and might reasonably hope to possess under the Crown great wealth and power. Their uncle, Anne de Montmorency, was Constable of France and had been a great influence with King Henry II. If we could enter into the minds of these three brothers and understand by what motives and through what channels they came to join the Huguenot movement, much light would be thrown on the obscure beginnings of French Protestantism. There can be no doubt of the sincerity with which they accepted the new faith. They exchanged the certainty of power and wealth for proscription and danger.

Odet when he abandoned the cardinal's red hat and the soaring chancel of the cathedral of Beauvais passed into comparative obscurity ; but his brother Gaspard became the greatest power in the councils of the Huguenots until he fell a victim in the massacre of Saint Bartholomew's Day. Before he made profession of the new faith he had commanded the armies of France, and it was due to his tenacity in defending Saint-Quentin that the Spanish armies were not able to make better use of the victory that they had won there and had not advanced straight upon Paris. Of all the statesmen who took the Protestant side in the sixteenth century Coligny was the most purely religious in his motives. He was by no means without fanaticism, and there was a sternness in his character which might easily pass into cruelty ; but, considering the standards of the times, his character is singularly free from stain. Coligny's name is naturally associated with those of Cromwell and William the Silent. He did not attain the success that came to the others, but he was not inferior to them in ability or in nobility of character.

Another family of even higher station was also closely connected with the Huguenot movement. The House of Bourbon was the very greatest of the old feudal families of France, though a heavy blow had been struck against it by Francis I when he had driven into exile the Constable and had confiscated his estates. No one could foresee that this house would before the end of the century give a King to France ; for seven of Catherine's ten children survived. But the Bourbons had already won a royal title by the marriage of Antony, Duke of Bourbon, to the Queen of Navarre. He became thus titular King of this fragment of a once larger state, seated on the north side of the Pyrenees and much coveted by the Kings of Spain. The Queen of Navarre was a passionate Calvinist and her influence brought her husband over to the same side. But the Protestant cause gained little or nothing from his support. He was unstable and lukewarm and his religious policy was evidently a by-product of his ambition. His son Henry—destined as Henry of Navarre to champion the Huguenot cause so boldly and to save it from destruction, and then as King Henry IV to desert it, but not before he had given it what seemed a safe legal position in France—was born in 1553. He inherited much of the qualities of both his parents but never had anything of the intensity of his mother's faith. King Antony had a brother Louis, Duke of Condé ; and he too was intimately associated with the Huguenots, for he had become recognized as " Protector of the Reformed Churches." The Huguenots had at first met obscurely and had concealed themselves as far as possible from public notice. But their numbers had been growing of late rapidly, and they were a force of importance even for politicians. Many of the nobility had joined them, and there were districts where they were in such force that they laid hands on the churches and used them for their own worship. But persecution had not slackened during the reign of Henry II, and they needed some system of defence. It was inevitable that the noble members of the confession should take the lead and thus the Protectorate of Condé was recognized. It was a natural move, but led to results of a questionable kind. Political aims and influences played a great part in the councils of the party. Soon they became connected with all the intricacies of foreign policy and were branded by their opponents as unpatriotic and anti-national.

The hopes of the Huguenots were high when the splinter of a spear stretched Henry II on the lists at Paris (1559). Calvin believed that if his preachers had free scope they would overthrow the ancient Church by the force of their arguments and the example of their life. The Huguenots had so grown in self-confidence that they gave to their movement a definite organization. The Genevan model was followed as far as possible, but many divergences were made necessary by the existence of a state, strong, alien, and hostile. At first each congregation was left very much to itself, though in each there was usually a minister and a " consistory " after the Genevan model. But in 1559 it was found necessary to call a General Synod of the whole Reformed Church in France and seventy-two churches were there represented. They made an address to the King and drew up a Confession of faith and rules of discipline. In the address to the King they professed themselves loyal and law-abiding subjects ; they appealed to the letter of the Scriptures in support of their doctrines and asked for permission to hold meetings for worship and the administration of sacraments. The Confession followed the Genevan model. It recognized no other authority than that of the canonical Scriptures; denounced papal corruptions on the one side and independent sectaries on the other; insisted with an almost Roman severity on the unity of the Church. "Wherever God shall have established a rightly ordered church—all who do not submit to it or who separate themselves from it are resisting the ordinance of God." At the same time a constitution was drawn up for the Church; the method of the appointment of ministers, elders, and deacons was laid down. The government of the Church was committed to local consistories and to provincial and national synods. Loyalty to the Crown and to all constituted authorities was promised. But no state in Europe in the sixteenth century could fail to regard with alarm this new and compact organization. The tendency of the age was for the state to take more and more of the functions of the Church under its own control. Here was a direct challenge to the authority of the state; a large and important part of the life of a body of subjects was withdrawn from it. Not until the nineteenth century was the possibility of such an arrangement recognized: and to-day in Italy, Germany and elsewhere there is a strong reaction against it. In the sixteenth century it inevitably led to civil war.

And yet attempts were made to find a road to peace. The Queen Mother hated the notion of war, for it would tend to make her own control of the government more difficult to maintain. She chose L'Hôpital to be her chancellor ; and he was not only famed for his humanity but closely connected with the Huguenots, though he remained himself in the Roman communion. An edict had already been issued suspending prosecutions for religious differences. A later edict mitigated the procedure and penalties for heresy.

But these efforts after peace were made in an atmosphere very unfavourable to them. Hardly any incidents are more obscure than those of the year 1560. Certainly the leaders of the Huguenots seem to have been more responsible for the disturbances than the government, which sincerely desired a pacification. First there came the strange affair known as the Tumult of Amboise. There were secret meetings addressed by a Huguenot noble, La Renaudie, who spoke of a greater captain who remained for the present in the background. Armed men gathered and made for the castle of Amboise where the royal family was residing. There is not much doubt that the aim of the movement was to make Condé ruler of France, without deposing the young King, and to introduce some regime favourable to the ideas of the Huguenots. But all was ill managed and the secret was not kept. The government struck and the movement was suppressed with much severity.

Still the Queen persevered. She called a meeting of Notables—royal nominees without constitutional powers—and asked them to suggest measures of conciliation. Coligny had been opposed to the Tumult of Amboise and took part in

31

the Assembly of Notables. There was a general agreement that the States-General, the traditional Parliament of France, should be summoned and that a Church Council should be called for the consideration of the claims of the Huguenots.

But the wilder section among the Huguenots believed that more could be done by a bold stroke. There were rumours of some movement in the south of France under the King of Navarre and Condé which might lead to the independence of that district. The leaders had been summoned to Court but had refused to comply. A more peremptory summons was obeyed. On his arrival Condé was arrested, tried, and condemned to death ; the King of Navarre was saved by an abject surrender. But Condé was not executed. The King had been ailing from his accession and died in December 1561. His successor, Charles IX, was a minor and the Queen Mother was now Regent in name as well as fact.

She still dreamed of peace by agreement. There is no reason at all for questioning her good faith ; but the country was in an uproar. The government had no force capable of maintaining order, and men's passions were too fierce for compromise. Still Catherine went on with her plans. The States-General were called at Orleans and L'Hôpital urged the claims of Christian unity. The States-General adjourned to Pontoise, and delegated their plenary functions to a committee of twenty-six. This smaller body was full of hostility to the reigning Church and urged the confiscation of Church property.   Then there was called a religious Council of all beliefs to Poissy (" The Colloquy of Poissy "). There was much debate but no agreement.   Notable figures appeared there :   Beza, Cardinal Guise, Peter Martyr, Lainez the Jesuit.   The gap between the Huguenots and their opponents was rather widened than bridged by the debate.

If States-General and religious colloquies could find no road to peace the government must act on its own authority, for the power of legislation was unquestionably in its hands.   So there came in January 1562 the Edict of January.   It is the first draught of the many edicts of toleration which the next thirty years were to see, and it leads up to the Edict of Nantes.   In the light of later events there is something almost amusingly simple in its stipulations.   The Huguenots may meet for worship outside of the towns ;   they must admit royal officials to their gatherings ;   they must preach nothing contrary to the Nicene Creed and the Scriptures.

While Catherine and L'Hôpital talked of peace men on both sides made them ready for battle. On March 1, 1562, Duke Francis of Guise was passing through Vassy on his road from the frontier and found a Huguenot service in progress there, though it was not within the district covered by the Edict of January.   He sent to protest and his soldiers were resisted.   In the scuffle that followed many lives were lost.   This small affair is known to history as the Massacre of Vassy and it marked the beginning of the religious wars.

CHAPTER II

THE RELIGIOUS WARS OF FRANCE

I CAN make no attempt to tell the story of the Religious Wars of France in this little volume. They influenced of course the development of the Huguenots profoundly, and the religious history of France is unintelligible without some knowledge of them. But they are peculiarly difficult to summarize. For thirty years France was torn by these civil contests, or at best rested from war without abandoning arms or enjoying any settled peace. There were no really decisive battles ; and, until the rise of Henry of Navarre, the wars produced no great soldier. The destruction to life and property was enormous and may be compared to what France had suffered during the Hundred Years' War with England, or what Germany suffered in the next century in her Thirty Years' War. All that can be done here is to mark the general character of the war, its decisive stages, the part played by the Huguenots and the influence of the war on their position and organization.

The government of France was until nearly the end strangely weak and nerveless. The French army had done great things against England, in

Italy, and against the Spaniards. If the Kings of France had possessed a force sufficient to make them masters in their own country France would have been spared many crimes and horrors, and in the last two reigns little difficulty had been experienced in raising a powerful army. But until the rise of Henry of Navarre there was no strong government in France. Many causes contributed to the weakness of the central authority. Many of the great nobles, the main support of the army and the agency by which the armies were collected, were now rebels. The Huguenot organizations were powerful and dangerous. But the chief cause, especially at first, was to be found in the character and aims of the Queen Mother and Regent, Catherine de Médicis. She was anxious to settle the religious controversy by conciliation and believed it could be done ; she feared war because she knew that war would exalt a soldier to power and would make the rule of a woman difficult or impossible. When war came she always embraced the first opportunity of making a settlement, however unstable it was bound to be. However strong be the popular legend to the contrary it is certain that she was not by nature cruel ; L'Hôpital had called her the kindest woman on earth. She had no long views. She fought and she massacred when it seemed politically expedient ; but when a breathing-space came her one idea was to induce the warring creeds to live on some amicable terms together. There are seven religious peaces during the thirty years of war, and all those bear the mark of her influence, even when they are not directly negotiated by her. It was not likely therefore that she would devote her energies to building up a strong military organization that might hold up the authority of the Crown against all rivals.

Both sides depended on foreign mercenaries to a surprising extent ; but the royal government was best able to hire them. Francis I had been proud of his national militia, and the victory of Marignano had been won by a predominantly French army ; but now foreigners, and especially Germans and Swiss, were hired to fight and ravage in the fields of France. One reason for preferring foreign to native troops was that when they were paid off they were done with. They did not interfere in the government or claim to control the religious policy of the state. The Huguenot armies had as a rule far more interest in the struggle than their opponents. Their tie to their aristocratic leaders was a personal one. They gathered and disappeared with surprising rapidity, in a way which reminds us of the Scotch clans in the seventeenth and eighteenth centuries, or of the Boers, some of them descendants of these very Huguenots, in the war of 1899–1901. After a defeat the Huguenot army was sometimes completely broken up and the royal forces seemed without opponents ; but in a few months we hear of Huguenot armies once more in the field. Nor was it easy to keep them together after a victory. There are much-disputed incidents in Henry of Navarre's career which are best explained by remembering that after a victory his men wanted to get home with their booty.

From 1562 to 1570 the war continued with two short " Peaces " which settled nothing. During these years the leadership of the Huguenots had changed. The King of Navarre's death during the first war was no loss to the Huguenots, for he was unstable alike in character and policy. His brother, the Duke of Condé, was more genuine in his adhesion to Calvinism, but he was deep in political intrigue, and though his death in battle left the Huguenots for a time leaderless, it was really a gain to them, for the first place in their councils and the leadership in their campaigns fell to Coligny. He was a fine leader of men, daring in the field, undaunted in defeat. Most important of all he was wholly devoted to the Huguenot cause. He was an ardent patriot, but religion came first and politics and patriotism were subordinate to what he believed was the true faith. All good causes were for him summed up in the triumph of the Gospel, and he believed that in foreign policy might be found a means of uniting the state, of giving a position of freedom and influence to the Huguenots, and of gaining for France an extension of her territory on her frontiers and an ascendancy in the councils of Europe. For from 1567 Philip of Spain was at war with his rebellious subjects in the Netherlands, and the struggle which was, to begin with, nationalist in its motive soon took a decided religious character. It was the settled aim of Coligny that France should resume

37

the struggle against Spain which had been brought
to an end by the Peace of Cateau-Cambrésis in
1559 ; that she should join hands with all the
Protestant powers everywhere who saw in Philip
their greatest enemy, but especially with the rebels
in the Netherlands. He saw in such a policy the
chance of striking a deadly blow against the papal
power and of winning for France important terri-
torial gains on her northern frontier and elsewhere.
And inevitably such a policy would give the Huguenots a position of freedom and influence in France ;
and he probably hoped that influence would grow
to power. From the death of Condé Coligny was
the chief influence among the Huguenots, but a
man destined to even greater fame had also appeared
in their ranks. At the beginning of the third civil
war (1568) the Queen of Navarre brought her son,
Henry, and placed him under the protection of
the Huguenots, who from that date made La
Rochelle their headquarters. Henry was born
in 1553 ; some years would therefore have to pass
before his influence could count for much with
the Huguenots ; but they were glad to have a
Prince of the Blood in their ranks, and it soon
became apparent that he had much more than his
name and his birth in his favour.

The Royalists as well as the Huguenots had
suffered change of leadership during these years.
Duke Francis of Guise had at first been the un-
questioned chief, but in 1563 he had been assassinated before the walls of Orleans, and his family
always firmly believed that the deed had been

38

instigated by Coligny. Coligny admitted that he had rejoiced at the death of one who was the greatest enemy of all that he most valued, but he denied that he had known of or in any way approved of the murder, and there can be no real doubt that he was telling the simple truth. There was no obvious or satisfactory successor. Montmorency was old and lukewarm in the Catholic cause and he was killed in 1568. The last campaigns were nominally conducted by the Queen's third son, the Duke of Anjou, and he won reputation and popularity from the battles of Jarnac and Moncontour. The young Henry of Guise, the son of the murdered Duke Francis, had distinguished himself at the siege of Poitiers and was already marked for popularity and high command ; but his time was not yet.

In 1570 came, not indeed a lasting peace, but a real breathing-space, which might turn into a real settlement of the religious controversies. The Queen negotiated the Peace of Saint-Germain, which gave the Huguenots much the same terms as had been accorded to them by the earlier peaces and is a direct forerunner of the Edict of Nantes. They were to have complete freedom of conscience ; that is to say, there was to be no inquisition to inquire into their secret thoughts and to make them incriminate themselves by cross-examination. Further, they were to have freedom of worship in the houses of the great nobles—a most significant concession—and in certain towns set apart in each administrative district. Then came the political provisions : the Huguenots were given right of appeal from the violently anti-Protestant Parlement of Toulouse and the right of protest against a certain number of judges in other Parlements. Lastly—and perhaps most important of all—they were to have the right of garrisoning and holding four strong towns—La Rochelle, Montauban, Cognac and La Charité. These provisions are remarkable. No religious dissidents in western Europe were so well treated as the Huguenots in France if these terms were observed. But many dangers threatened. There was no appeasement at all in men's minds : no moral disarmament. Each side regarded the other as the representative and the agent of Evil, as the enemy of social and political order and the cause of damnation hereafter. Until those passions died down mutual toleration was nearly impossible. The provisions of the Peace too about the Parlements and the guarantee towns conflicted with the strong and growing feeling for the unity of the state and the equality of all men before the law. For under the Edict there were strong towns where the King did not rule and courts where some Frenchmen had privileges which others did not possess.

Coligny hoped to give the settlement a measure of stability and enlargement through a change in foreign policy. Between the Peace of Saint-Germain in August 1570 and the Massacre of Saint Bartholomew's Day on August 24, 1572, an immense and decisive change seemed possible in the foreign policy of France and the relations of the great powers. The King, Charles IX, the least contemptible of the sons of Catherine, was growing to manhood and he was inclined to follow an independent line of policy and a little resentful of his mother's interference. He saw much of Coligny and was attracted by him. He was won over to an acceptance of the grandiose plans of the Huguenot leader. War with Spain and alliance with the Protestant powers, especially with England ; the alliance to be cemented by royal marriages ; the war to be opened by an expedition to the Netherlands where the nationalist and Protestant party was at present crushed by the army of Alva but was ready to rise at the first opportunity—these were the outlines of Coligny's scheme and to these the King inclined to give his consent. Such a policy was a continuation of the international strategy of Francis I and Henry II, and an anticipation of that which in the hands of Richelieu and Mazarin gave France a decided ascendancy in Europe for a century. For a time all seemed to Coligny to be going well, though there could be no doubt as to the dangers and difficulties that lay ahead. The proposal to marry Henry of Anjou —Catherine's favourite son—to Elizabeth of England broke down. But though there was to be no Anglo-French marriage an Anglo-French treaty was signed at Blois in April 1572, whereby each country promised assistance to the other in case of attack from whatever quarter. The Treaty of Blois has no great name in history, but the *entente* thus established between the two countries was a main cause of the success of the foreign policy of Elizabethan England. It was equally important to the Kings of France and was unshaken even by the Great Massacre and the renewal of the civil-religious wars. Another marriage was successfully arranged. Henry of Navarre was not yet the heir to the French throne, nor did there seem much likelihood of his ever being so, but he was a Prince and the most exalted name among the Huguenots. It was arranged that he should marry Margaret of Valois, the King's sister. Jeanne d'Albret, the Queen of Navarre, came to Paris to make arrangements for the marriage. The sincere Huguenot lady was shocked by the corruption of the Court, but was determined to win so great a connexion for her son. She died before the marriage took place ; but on August 18, 1572, the marriage was celebrated in Notre Dame Cathedral.

There was great news too from the Netherlands. The growing national spirit, in alliance with Protestant zeal and commercial indignation against the financial oppression of the Spaniards, had provided excellent material for diplomatic intrigue to work on. On April 1 Brill had been taken by the Water Beggars, as the sailor exiles of Holland were called, or more truly had been surrendered to them. The movement spread rapidly over the rich provinces of Holland and Zealand and the adjacent districts. William of Orange, the exiled leader of the national party, came from his German lands to take command of the movement. Until his death thirteen years later he was the most prominent leader among the Calvinists of Europe. He was as cautious as he was brave and had at first questioned the wisdom of the rising in the Netherlands. When he joined himself to it and became its leader his chief reliance was on the assistance which was confidently expected from France. He and Coligny would have been perfect co-operators in a great war against Spain.

France had not declared war against Spain, but a military expedition was being undertaken with the approval of the government. Alva was laying siege to Mons. A French force, mainly consisting of Huguenots under Genlis, marched to its relief. If France threw herself heartily into the struggle Alva would be caught between two fires and would be in great danger.

Instead there came the Massacre of Saint Bartholomew's Day, the withdrawal of all support from the Dutch rebels, the resumption of the miserable series of the religious wars. I can only give what I believe to be far the most probable explanation of the tragic event. The idea of sweeping off the Huguenots by some sudden blow was familiar to men's minds ; the Guise family were quite prepared to take their share in such a policy. Catherine de Médicis would have no scruples about reaching her political ends by means of massacre ; moral scruples were at no time a trouble to her. But her whole policy had been aimed at conciliation with the Huguenots. It was she who had appointed L'Hôpital Chancellor ;

it was she who had negotiated the three Peaces of religious toleration. She had been at one time in alliance with Coligny and was heartily disliked for her religious opportunism at Rome and Madrid. The idea that the Massacre was a deep-laid plan inspired by religious hatred and that even the marriage proposals of the year were merely baits to entice the Huguenots into the trap may be dismissed as impossible. Catherine had welcomed the prospect of religious appeasement, I believe, sincerely—more sincerely than perhaps anyone in France because religious passions had no hold on her. But as the international situation developed it came to have many features which alarmed her. She loved power—it was the master passion of the latter part of her life—and power seemed slipping from her hands into those of this masterful Coligny. She loved peace if only because during war power must fall into the hands of a man ; and here was war coming, war on a far greater scale than the struggle against the Huguenots, war against a Catholic power, war against the admired and dreaded power of Spain, war against her own son-in-law, Philip II. If war brought victory quickly there would be compensations. But would it ? The force of Frenchmen who went to the relief of Mons was defeated with ignominious ease. Fear came upon her, says a contemporary, because of the armies of Spain ; and with fear a willingness to employ cruelty to escape from the trap that seemed closing in on her. Paris was full of Huguenots who had come up for Henry of Navarre's wedding.

They were very unpopular with the people of Paris. If the government gave the lead there would be plenty of willing hands to join in the killing of the hated sectaries.

It is impossible to free Catherine from the chief responsibility for the horrible crime which followed. She was warmly seconded by the Guises ; but it was she who persuaded or terrorized the weak King into acquiescence. The signal was given, though not by the fabled shot fired from the windows of the Louvre. Henry of Guise superintended in person the murder of Coligny, whom he had always regarded as his father's assassin. The Parisians hunted the Huguenots in every street in Paris and the example of the capital was imitated in many provincial towns. Certainly thousands perished, but no estimate of the number of victims is based on evidence of much value.

The most amazing thing about this atrocious crime is that it produced so little result except in the sphere of foreign affairs. There it was a real thunder-stroke. France withdrew from the projected alliance with the nationalist rising in the Netherlands, and William the Silent was left to fight on in what looked at first a hopeless cause ; his heroic struggle, his death and the ultimate partial triumph of the movement to which he gave his life must not even be glanced at. But the alliance or *entente* with England was maintained ; and in France after a short time the chief currents flowed much as before. There was first another spasm of civil war, in which the Huguenots with diminished numbers held on stoutly behind the water-defences of La Rochelle; and in a few months the government gave them a peace of the usual kind, though the terms were by no means so generous as had been accorded by the Peace of Saint-Germain, or as were soon to be given them in other treaties. But by the Peace of La Rochelle freedom of conscience was conceded and a closely restricted right of Protestant worship. Considerations of foreign policy had played a part in deciding the government to grant these terms.

Charles IX died in 1574. He was succeeded by his brother, Henry III, who was called home from Poland where he had been elected to the throne. He is the strangest figure in this age in which we so often seem to be in the atmosphere of a lunatic asylum. A charming statuette in the Wallace collection in London presents to us a by no means displeasing face. In early youth he was considered to have military ambitions and abilities, but all that vanished. He had the traditional royal passion for the chase, but he seems to have had little real interest in public affairs. He was constant and superstitious in religious practices, many of which were devoted to praying for the birth of a son and heir who never arrived. It is quite likely that his brain and will and character—none of them very strong—broke under the strain of a situation which would have tried the strongest nerves and the keenest intellect. There came another religious war when he arrived in France. It was brought to an end by the Peace of Monsieur (1576) which is one of the most remarkable documents which the century produced in any country.

For the Peace of Monsieur declared without any qualification the principle of religious equality. The Huguenots were to worship where and how they liked (though there were certain not really important limitations in the interests of public order) ; they were to possess complete civil equality and to be admissible to all careers. As a guarantee of the good faith of the government ten important towns were put in their keeping and they were to have legal protection in the Parlements by the appointment of many Huguenot judges. The Huguenots had thus got from the Queen Mother and her son—both of them deeply implicated in the Massacre—all that they could fairly demand, and more than was given to them by their King, Henry of Navarre, when at last he mounted the French throne. How was such a result made possible ?

First, I insist, by the easy-going nature of the Queen and by her belief in the possibility of religious peace. And next by a change in the grouping of parties at home. The spectacle of the massacre and of the constant wars had not left the people of France unmoved. A new party—the Politiques —had arisen and had secured the adhesion of the King's only surviving brother, the Duke of Alençon. The ultimate settlement of France came from this party, or at any rate was in harmony with the feelings of this party. In brief, they put the interests of the state and people above the rivalries of the two creeds. They were not irreligious men—some of them were very pious. They were Catholics and as such repudiated the system and the discipline of Geneva. They desired the unity of the state, and they believed that it could be gained by giving the Huguenots a position of security and that it could not be gained by exterminating them or by proscribing their worship. Catherine de Médicis was essentially a Politique ; so was Queen Elizabeth ; so in his heart of hearts was William the Silent ; so was Henry of Navarre both before and after his " conversion." To all of them religious controversy was a secondary matter, though an important one ; victory in that field, they thought, would be dearly purchased by the confusion or the weakening of the state.

But there was a strong and large section of the French people to whom the idea of tolerating the poison of heresy was hateful. The intellectual basis of religious liberty had been little thought out and had never been declared with any persuasiveness. When a large section of the nobles and people of France were entering into alliance with the Huguenots it was time for those whose adhesion to the Roman Church was ardent and unqualified to bestir themselves. So there grew up the Catholic League. There had been early movements of the same kind, but the full-grown League was the product of the Peace of Monsieur. The League clearly aimed at the expulsion of Calvinism from France and it subordinated everything, even patriotism, to the maintenance of the purity of the faith. Its political objects were secondary to its religious aims, but it was strongly aristocratic in character. It desired to see the calling of the States-General and the re-establishment of the liberties of France " as they were in the time of King Clovis." While the League found its political ideals in the seventh century it showed itself aware of the actual forces of its own time by making Philip of Spain Protector of the League. He accepted the position with readiness and saw in it a possible means, not merely of weakening the hostility of France, but even of acquiring the French throne for himself or for some member of his family.

For in 1584 the death of a very poor creature profoundly affected the situation in France. Catherine had had ten children, but there was no heir to the throne except her own sons. The eager hope that a son might be born to Henry III was not realized. If he died—and like all Catherine's sons he was weakly—the next heir was his brother, the Duke of Alençon. He cannot be credited with any ability, but his relation to the throne gave him great importance. For this reason there had been marriage negotiations with Elizabeth of England in spite of the wide disparity of their ages ; in 1583 Elizabeth was 50 and Alençon 29. For this reason, too, William the Silent had persisted in offering him the Protectorship of the free Netherlands with the title of Prince, and had repeated his offer when the Duke's treasonous intentions were apparent to all the world. But in 1584 he died.

And now who was heir to the throne of France ? If we try to understand the genealogical table of the Bourbons and Valois it is hard to convince ourselves that Henry of Navarre was the rightful heir. But such was undoubtedly the fact ; for even the Catholic League, though it passed him over as a heretic, adopted his uncle, Cardinal Bourbon, as its candidate for the throne. If the rules which by law and tradition governed the succession to the Crown of France were allowed to operate a Huguenot Prince would become King of France. But would legal rules be allowed to operate ? The Catholic League answered with a decided No. They developed a theory of the divine right of Kings—the very opposite of the doctrine which later passed under that name in England—and maintained that the King of France must of necessity be in communion with Rome. If so, Henry of Navarre could not reign. The Cardinal Bourbon might be safely accepted for the time being, for he was old and childless. But when he died ? There all was obscure. Certainly the Guises thought that their claims ought to be considered and busily worked at their pedigree until it connected them with Charlemagne. But the League tightened the bonds which united it with Philip II of Spain. Why should not he succeed ? If the line of legitimate succession were broken ought not the house of Valois to be pushed right aside ? And after all Philip was closely connected with the royal family by marriage. But if he was not acceptable some relation might be found who would bring the strength of Spain to the support of Catholicism in France and incidentally would harness France to the chariot of Spain.

The Huguenots, whose existence was responsible for all this confusion of thought and action, had not relaxed their organization nor weakened in their devotion to the ideas of Calvin. They had shown endurance and high military qualities in the wars and it was becoming clear that they could not be reduced by a merely military repression. Henry of Navarre from being an attractive head had become a real leader. On the night of the massacre he had abjured his faith to save his life, but he had taken an early opportunity of rejoining the Huguenot army and once more professing its faith. He was already beginning to catch the imagination of France. He was young, handsome, brave, gallant ; a most welcome contrast to the kings and princes of the Valois line. He was more than this ; he was a subtle and penetrating states-man, full of craft and personal ambition ; but there had not yet been time to develop this side of him nor to exhibit his great military gifts.

Henry of Navarre was well served and had the gift of winning the affection and loyalty of his servants. The first place among them must be accorded to the Duke of Sully. We know him well through his *Mémoires*, of which we shall have to speak again in the next chapter. This strange, and by no means always trustworthy book, is the most precious popular document for the history of the time. The Duke was several years younger than his master, whom he followed faithfully to the end of his reign. He reveals himself in his *Mémoires* as by no means a strict Puritan in his morals and manners, but he remained loyal to the Calvinist Church in spite of strong temptations to follow his master in a change of religious confession. He shared the military perils of the Huguenot armies and was badly wounded at the battle of Ivry, but his chief value to Henry was not in the battle-field. He was primarily a statesman and financier, shrewd, realistic and not too scrupulous ; humorous, strong-willed, and by no means averse from finding his own advantage in the confusions of the time. King and Minister were in these two men admirably suited. A very different type of Huguenot noble was du Plessis-Mornay, whose interests were more religious than political and who has left a long series of works on the controversies of the day. His adhesion to Henry of Navarre was unquestionable, and he defended his claims to the throne of France with his pen as well as with his sword. He ranks too among the original political thinkers of the age. There were many other notable Huguenots ; but it must be noted that since the formation of the Politique party Henry could count on the support of very many, both nobles and commoners, who were not Huguenots. His strength lay in the stubborn devotion of the Huguenot party and in his alliance with the Politiques.

The death of the Duke of Alençon in 1584 broke the uneasy peace which had existed for some years and produced a new war of a kind different from what had gone before. On the one side was the Catholic League, backed by Philip of Spain and the influence of the Papacy, and led by Henry of Guise, whose gallantry and popularity were great and growing. On the other side was Henry and his politique associates who defended the strictly hereditary character of the French Crown, for that meant the accession of Henry of Navarre to the throne of France, and supported a settlement of religion on a basis of toleration and arrangement. The aims of the Catholic League and of the Huguenots and Politiques were clear ; but what was King Henry III going to do ? The control of events was slipping from his nerveless fingers. There can be little doubt that he and his mother leaned rather to the side of the Politiques than of the League. He issued a manifesto deploring the manifold evils which a war was bound to bring to France. But the passions of men were too highly inflamed to be appeased by thoughts of the consequences of war ; and when war came Henry III took the side of the League. " The War of the Three Henries " is the name given to the next phase of the Religious Wars of France, but it is better called the War of the Catholic League. Henry III played a subordinate part ; he soon saw his worst enemy in the leader of the League, Henry of Guise, and got rid of him in a way characteristic of the decadent Valois.

In the war, Henry of Navarre won one important battle—Coutras—in October 1587. Henry of Guise won a battle equally important against German mercenaries who were marching to the help of Henry of Navarre and who were crushed by Guise at Auneau in November 1587. The King sank into insignificance between these two gallant combatants. Especially in Paris Henry of Guise— " The King of the League "—was the hero of the hour, while the King himself was suspected of lukewarmness in the cause. When Guise approached Paris after his victory at Auneau the city prepared to give him an enthusiastic welcome ; and, though the King forbade him to enter, he entered and was greeted with passionate enthusiasm. The King felt himself in danger and fled from Paris. But even outside of Paris there was no means of escaping the dominion of the King of the League. Henry III had to sign the Edict of Union whereby he promised to make no peace with the Huguenots, and a little later he made Guise Lieutenant-General of the Kingdom. The King seemed to be slipping into the position of the merest *roi fainéant*.

But though the King could not fight with any vigour there was another weapon which he might perhaps handle with success. The situation is not altogether unlike what it had been on the eve of the Saint Bartholomew's Day Massacre. As Coligny then threatened the power and influence of the Queen Mother so now her son found himself overshadowed by Guise. He too used assassination to escape the toils that seemed closing round him, and at first he had greater success than had attended the plans of his mother. The League had insisted on the summons of the States-General to Blois. No Huguenots and few Politiques were there. The League was everything and the King was a shadow by the side of Guise. But on December 23 the King invited him to his private apartment and there had him murdered. His brother the Cardinal was soon murdered too. Henry III believed that he had made himself really King of France; but he soon found that he was " King of Nothing." The League repudiated him; the Church through the theological Faculty of Paris repudiated him; Paris repudiated him. To whom could he turn for any hope of safety? The Huguenot-Politique party proclaimed the indefeasible right of the legitimate heir to the Crown, and Henry of Navarre was ready to forget the past (though there were incidents in that past that were difficult to forget). The two surviving Henrics met at Plessis-les-Tours and made a close alliance. It is noteworthy that a manifesto from Henry of Navarre spoke of " conversion " as though it were not outside of the bounds of possibility, though he refused to yield to compulsion.

The alliance was a great success. The King and the rightful heir to the throne won the adhesion of many elements in the state. The League was powerful, especially in Paris and some other large towns. But it was now definitely anti-national and even pro-Spanish in its character, and France seemed to rally to the national monarchy. The army of the League could not resist the joint forces of the two Henries, and in the summer of 1589 they advanced on Paris and the fall of the great city seemed certain. Famine was sore within the walls. There was no possibility of a relieving force. If Paris fell the claims of Henry of Navarre to the succession would be universally recognized and some religious settlement would be introduced. But on August 2, 1589, a friar made his way from Paris into the royal camp on the pretext that he was bringing news from the beleaguered city, and being introduced into the presence of Henry III stabbed him with a fatal wound.

One Henry alone remained. He was extremely popular and he was the legal heir to the throne. But he was a heretic ! On the one side the peace of France under a ruler whom most people admired ; on the other the stain of heresy. Which consideration would carry most weight ? It was soon apparent that France would not willingly be ruled over by any but a member of the Roman Catholic Church. Henry had to break up the leaguer of Paris and was again an adventurer fighting for the Crown.

He won the open support of Elizabeth of England, and English money and support were of great service to him. Soon a complete victory seemed within his grasp. He won two great battles— Arques and Ivry—and then pressed on a second time to the siege of Paris. And again the surrender of the great city seemed certain. In a very short time famine must do its fatal work, and Henry would reign without abjuration of his faith. But if Elizabeth gave open help to Henry that was a reason why Philip should throw the sword of Spain into the opposite scale. And the sword of Spain was wielded by Parma, the greatest soldier of the century. Paris was saved from the Huguenot in 1590, and Rouen was saved by the same great soldier in the next year. Henry, it was clear, would not win secure possession of the Crown by the sword alone, and he would not reign over a united France as a Huguenot.

His conversion had been canvassed for years past. And it is difficult to condemn it. His adhesion to Calvinism was probably genuine, but it was not primarily religious nor was it theological at all. He disliked the idea of leaving his old comrades-in-arms, who had fought for him for so long and whose support had brought him so near to the throne. But the *Institutes of the Christian Religion* can have meant little to him and the discipline of Geneva had never appealed to him. Indeed, Henry of Navarre among the Huguenots presents the same sort of almost comic contrast as his grandson, Charles II of England, when in 1650 he signed the Covenant and professed to obey the behests of the Congregation in Scotland. (Charles II had much of his grandfather in his constitution, though no trace of his military ability.) To Henry of Navarre the question was primarily a political one. Even Sully, though he refused to follow his master in his conversion, did not dissuade it and foretold the appeasement that it would bring to France.

A conference with the leaders of the League was

opened at Surène. The conversion of the King was then seen to be a certainty ; but Henry was anxious to be received into the Church without accepting papal absolution, and to make it clear that his view of the Church was that of the nationalists and Gallicans. Then came his " instruction " at the hands of four Bishops. On Sunday, July 25, he was admitted into the Cathedral of Saint-Denis. He was crowned at Chartres and a little later received papal absolution.

The success of the step in all that Henry most valued was soon apparent. The nobility and the cities of France eagerly embraced the excuse to abandon their resistance to the King. Paris resisted longer, for Paris had received a Spanish garrison : but even Paris surrendered at last and when the King rode through the streets the people seemed mad with joy " to look again upon the face of a King." The Huguenots did not share in the national jubilation. There was among them a large proportion of men and women to whom their religion was much more than a matter of expediency and who regarded the King's conversion as a great apostasy which would receive divine punishment. Of them we must speak in the next chapter, but we may note here that many of the old Huguenots refused to co-operate with the King in his later struggles.

And his struggles were not completely over by any means when he had entered Paris. The hope that had gleamed before the eyes of Philip II— that he might win the Crown of France either for

himself or for some near and obedient relative—
was too fascinating to be lightly dismissed. So
when the civil war ended open war with Spain still
continued, and here Henry suffered more than one
annoying check at the hands of the Spanish troops.
Especially was he exasperated by the fall of Amiens
and inclined to blame Huguenot lukewarmness
for the temporary loss of this great fortress and
city. Henry had once told Sully that chief among
his hopes was that he might one day win a great
victory against the Spaniards ; but that hope was
never realized. The organization of the Spanish
army was superior to that of the French and the
troops had a national spirit and pride which the
French did not attain to until the next reign. So
the war dragged on without reaching any decisive
result, and in 1598 Henry made with Philip III
the Peace of Vervins. Its terms are not important
and in any case do not concern us. We must turn
to the Huguenots and their condition under Henry
IV.

CHAPTER III

It was natural that the Huguenots should be irritated with Henry IV. They had welcomed him as their leader long before he was heir to the French throne. They had fought for him with constant loyalty. They had dropped their early liberal political views in order to support his claim to the Crown on the ground of indefeasible hereditary right. They had carried him up to the steps of the throne. And then he had deserted them. The very strong arguments that can be adduced in defence of his action—his own very tepid adhesion to Calvinism, the terrible sufferings of France— naturally did not appeal to them. They only saw the apostasy, and in spite of all his promises feared that it might lead to some treacherous blow against their religious liberties. The promised settlement was long in coming. They watched his struggle against Spain, suspicious and morose, without giving him much help. But they were mistaken in their suspicions of him. His later relations to his Huguenot comrades are not free from regrettable incidents, but he all along intended to keep his promise to them. There had been enough attempted settlements in the past, which had promised well, but which had failed because they sprang only from good intentions and were not backed by an effective force. Henry IV knew enough of the realities of statecraft not to fall into the sentimental mistakes of Catherine de Médicis. He would attempt no settlement until he was master of France and until he could dictate his terms to his countrymen with the prestige of victory behind him.

The religious life of France was still governed by the various modifications which had been introduced into the Edict of Monsieur. The Peace of Bergerac in 1577 had declared for freedom of conscience and had given the Huguenots permission to worship in the houses of the great nobility and in one town in each administrative district. They held some nine fortresses as security for the observance of the terms, and they had the right to be tried by benches of judges containing Huguenots as well as Catholics. Henry's settlement in the Edict of Nantes is a development of this. It is certainly true, though not usually recognized, that he was but carrying on and placing on a firmer basis a policy that had been inaugurated by Catherine de Médicis. He himself fully admitted the connexion between the Edict of Nantes and the work of his predecessors on the throne. He told the Parlement of Paris that his edict really belonged to the " late King," that is Henry III. He might with even more truth have said that it was the work of

Catherine de Médicis. Henry of Navarre has been too highly praised for his services to religious liberty ; and the work of Catherine and her children has been too little recognized. They have been too usually regarded as bitter opponents, whereas they were really co-operators.

The King's relations with the Huguenots were dangerously strained in the five years that followed his abjuration. A new civil war was by no means impossible. There was much to alarm the Protestants. Henry's chief business was to win over to loyalty the nobles and cities who had taken the side of the League. He was anxious to do nothing that would recognize their corporate existence and therefore made separate treaties with individuals. He gave the ex-rebels good terms, and one of the terms was nearly always a promise that no Protestant service of any kind should be allowed in their neighbourhoods. The pay promised to the Huguenot garrisons in the guarantee towns was either not paid at all or curtailed. The King clearly made more of his new friends than of his old allies. The Huguenots determined to leave as little as possible to chance and could not feel themselves safe in the mere good intentions of the King. At Nantes they swore that they would live and die united in the confession of the Calvinist faith. They developed their organization. The whole country was divided into nine provinces each with its own council. Every year there was to be a general assembly, made up of deputies from the provinces, which was to deliberate on the general interests of the

Huguenot party. It was this organization which forced on the Edict of Nantes ; but it conflicted directly with those ideas of state unity, which had so strong a hold on the mind of France. It had a suspicious resemblance to those Leagues which in Germany had contributed so much to the disruption of the Empire. The nobles played a great part in the Councils of the Huguenots. They were doubtless welcome because of their influence with the King and their knowledge of public affairs. But their influence on Huguenot policy was by no means always a good one. They aroused the jealousy of the King and tended to mix their party up in questionable intrigues with foreign powers.

Henry was profoundly disappointed with the behaviour of the Huguenots when the Spaniards took Amiens by surprise (March 1597). He called on them for help, but they answered by a strong reaffirmation of their claims and sent little assistance. Sully was always with the King, but he had ceased to count for much with the Huguenots. La Trémoille and the Duke of Bouillon had raised troops, but refused to go to the King's assistance. When Amiens was retaken in 1597 it was clear that the religious situation would admit of no further delay.

The General Assembly of the Huguenots was sitting at Châtellerault. The King asked them to send him four deputies to arrange for a settlement. The Duke of Bouillon was associated with them. There was much hard negotiation before the end was reached. The protests of the Catholics had to be listened to. The Edict of Nantes is the result of mutual concessions and compromises. It has none of the clear statement of principles which makes the Edict of Monsieur so notable, but when it was issued it would be obeyed.

The Edict of Nantes owes its name to the fact that Henry signed it when he was on his way to the settlement of disturbances in Brittany. It was a curiously complicated document or rather series of documents. There was first the Edict proper in ninety-two articles. This was followed by fifty-six secret and private articles, which were, however, also registered by the Parlement of Paris. Then there were two commissions (*brevets*) dealing with the question of guarantees ; and then there came yet other " secret " articles. The greater part of the documents is taken up with the judicial stipulations and guarantees.

The preamble said that the settlement of religion had been held back by the need of dealing first with those questions which depended on force. The King had received numerous complaints from both Catholics and Huguenots, " and as God had not yet been pleased to allow France to enjoy one and the same form of religion " it was necessary to make regulations whereby the peace of the country might be maintained.

There was to be complete freedom of conscience. Huguenots might live anywhere " without being examined, harassed, or constrained to do anything contrary to their conscience."

They were not to have the unrestricted freedom

of worship promised by the Edict of 1576 ; but much was accorded to them. The great nobles might have Protestant worship in their houses for as many as they liked so long as they themselves were personally present. The smaller nobility were to be allowed to have Protestant worship, but only for their families ; though there is a vague clause added that on special occasions " such as baptisms, visits from friends, and others " there would be no objection to the presence of strangers up to the number of thirty. Further Calvinist worship might be held wherever " it was established and publicly celebrated in the years 1596 and 1597." A separate article says that such worship may also be held where it was established by the Edict of Pacification of the year 1577. Lastly, by another clause, in each of the seventy administrative districts of France (*bailliages* and *sénéchaussées*) one town was to be set apart for Protestant services and another town in each district was subsequently added by the secret articles. I shall comment on these concessions later.

Complete civil equality was promised. The Huguenots were not to be excluded from schools or universities or state employment or trades guilds or professions of any kind.

To secure the fair administration of justice special chambers were to be established in most of the Parlements ; sometimes these chambers were to be equally divided between Catholics and Protestants ; sometimes the division was to be rather less favourable to the Protestants.

The right of the Huguenots to self-government was stated with some obscurity. First all assemblies were dissolved ; all negotiations in the name of the whole party forbidden ; all collections of moneys or arms prohibited—except by permission of the King. But in the Secret Articles—which were not secret at all—meetings for religious purposes and for discipline, and also colloquies, consistories, and provincial and national synods were allowed. But here, too, after a protest from the Catholic clergy, a phrase was added—" by the permission of His Majesty." The simple-looking words turned out to be of great importance in the next century.

Lastly the *brevet* dealt with the very burning question of guarantee towns. The method of handling it is curiously vague and unsatisfactory. The Huguenots are allowed to maintain garrisons " in all towns and castles which they held up to August last " for the space of eight years. At the end of the eight years the Huguenot Governor is to be maintained if the garrison is still kept. Thus the number of towns in Huguenot hands is not given definitely, but the number of places is believed to amount to something like 100. Another clause in the brevet sets aside a sum of money which may be used for the payment of Huguenot pastors.

Complete freedom of conscience ; complete civil equality ; closely limited freedom of worship ; excellent guarantees for the administration of justice ; a large state subsidy for the maintenance of Huguenot troops and ministers : the Edict may perhaps be thus summed up.

It gave France a splendid period of religious peace during which she assumed the leadership in Europe in culture as well as in war and diplomacy. It has been greeted with a chorus of approval even by those who can see nothing to praise in the seven edicts which contained much the same provisions and which emanated from Catherine and her children. For the state in the hand of a strong ruler was behind the Edict now, and it would not for three generations be thrown on one side. The religious liberty that was thus given fully justified itself. The Huguenots took more than their proportional share in the development of commerce and industry which was soon to follow ; they were valuable as financiers and administrators ; they proved—when they had thrown off their connexion with the nobles —a peaceful and loyal section of the community. The Church in France profited by their presence in greater watchfulness and intellectual vigour. The age of Protestant liberty is also the golden age of the Gallican Church.

And yet the Edict hardly seems to deserve the unqualified eulogy which it has received from many quarters. It was a splendid stroke of statecraft and a measure of justice and humanity fully justified by the results. But it was far from an ideal settlement, and some of the trials and torments, which in the next century fell upon the Huguenots, are to be traced in part to its provisions. We will briefly note some of the defects of the Edict.

First it made the Huguenot Church far too dependent on the nobles. Their rights come first; their names are mentioned when those of the humbler negotiators of the Edict are forgotten. We are always liable to pay far too much attention to these aristocratic champions of the Huguenots and to neglect the humble bourgeois, the learned and sincere ministers, the ordinary congregations who met regularly for the administration of the sacraments, the singing of hymns, and the other forms in which they worshipped God. And yet these were the very foundation of the movement and without these men the noble protectors would have had no power. The nobles did often protect very really, but they also attracted the suspicion of the King; he knew them for his worst enemies in France and suspected their loyalty to the Crown and to France, and as the sequel was to show his suspicions were justified.

The provisions for worship were curiously unsatisfactory. The meetings in noble castles must have been unpropitious to the development of a movement the strength of which lay with the middle class. Two places of worship in a district about as large as the English County divisions of to-day offered very insufficient opportunities to a widely scattered community. All " temples "—for that is the official word for a Huguenot church—which existed in 1577, 1596, and 1597 were to be maintained. But what were those places? How was the existence of a Huguenot meeting to be proved? With good will on both sides no trouble need have arisen. But there was little good will from the first and soon there was a desire to interpret the Edict in the sense most hostile to the Huguenots.

The statement too that the meetings of the Huguenots for purposes of the administration and the government of their affairs could only be held " by permission of His Majesty " proved of more consequence than had at first seemed likely. What the King could permit, the King could forbid, and the Huguenots found themselves at the mercy of a Louis XIV for all except the conduct of their ordinary religious services.

All would have been well if there had been a strong body of opinion and conviction in favour of a settlement resting on liberty. But there were very few men or women in Europe in 1600 who believed that it was safe to leave religion to individual judgment. Most men believed that state unity depended on religious unity. When Pope Clement VIII told Henry's emissary in Rome that the Edict was the most accursed that could be imagined, " because by the Edict liberty of conscience was permitted to everyone and that was the worst thing in the world," he was misrepresenting the Edict—for it admitted only the possibility of two forms of religion in France—but his view was widely accepted even outside of his own communion. The Duke of Sully, the great Huguenot financier statesman, was of the same opinion. In his proposed rearrangement of Europe he would admit Lutheranism and Calvinism by the side of the Roman Catholic Church, but he would go no further : " there is nothing in all respects so pernicious," he wrote, " as a liberty in belief." Men talked much of religious liberty in the sixteenth century, but they meant usually liberty for their own form of religion to oppress the others. The Calvinists were not free from this charge in Geneva, or in the Netherlands, or in Scotland, or in England later ; there is no likelihood that if they had won the power in France they would have abstained from using it in support of their own faith and form of worship. The Edict of Nantes was not the product of theory but of necessity. The theory would come and in another century would gain a large success across the Channel. But it came too late to save the Huguenots.

It is curiously difficult to be sure of the numbers of the Huguenots in France at the end of the sixteenth century. An Italian contemporary says that Henry IV took a census of them in 1598 and that the total number was one million and a quarter ; that there were 951 churches, of which 257 were attached to the houses of noblemen. Perhaps this is a little in excess of the reality ; in any case the proportion of " noble " to public churches is interesting. They were widely but not uniformly scattered over France. Protestantism has sometimes been regarded as essentially a form of religion adapted to the northern peoples, but in France there were more Huguenots south than north of the Loire. The Rhône valley and the country between the mouths of the Loire and the Garonne were districts where they were to be found in great numbers. There were also many in Normandy. Orleans had been their stronghold at the beginning of the wars, but that had been taken from them. Their chief strongholds were now Nîmes, Montpellier, Montauban, and La Rochelle. Paris was always hostile to them, and they were not allowed to have a temple within its walls, but they had one in the suburb of Charenton capable of holding at least 4,000 worshippers.

We have had enough of Huguenot politics. It would be interesting to enter one of their many temples and see the type of worship established there. The buildings anticipated the English Nonconformist chapels of a later date. Here were no High Altars, no statues, no painted windows glowing with pictures of saints and Biblical characters ; the cross was not admitted even on the outside. The shape of the buildings was sometimes circular or oval but more usually rectangular. In the inside the most noteworthy features were the *parquet* or slightly raised platform on the one side, and the pulpit on the other. The members of the consistory and certain other officials of the church had the right to a seat on the parquet. Seats were also allotted to certain public personages on the floor ; among them to such members of the Roman Catholic Church as liked to attend, whose presence was a source of annoyance and sometimes of danger to the Huguenots. The pulpit was the most important part of the furnishing of the temple. Protestantism generally increased immensely the importance of the sermon ; but nowhere quite so much as in the Calvinist churches. The sermon was the essential part of their system ; and, though there were services without it, they were reputed less solemn than the others. It was laid down in their discipline that something in the nature of a sermon was necessary to give full validity to baptisms, marriages and the administration of the Communion. There was no rigidly fixed form of service, though the same general type was everywhere observed. Laymen whether as deacons, readers, or elders took a share in the service. The ministers and the male members of the congregation wore their hats, only removing them during specially solemn ceremonies ; such as the reading of the commandments and the creed and the administration of the Communion. The congregation repeated after the minister certain of the prayers ; the reading of the Bible played a large part in the services ; the psalms were much loved and constantly sung both in church and outside ; the singing of them in church was made obligatory upon all. The Communion of the Lord's Supper was administered four times a year and was obligatory on all members of the church. During the sixteenth and seventeenth centuries laymen shared in the handing of the elements to the communicants, who received them standing but hatless. None were admitted who did not possess a token, usually of metal, called a *méreau*, which had to be presented to the officials. On Sunday afternoons there was a service called a catechism. What was called the Grand Catechisme took the form of questions put from the pulpit to the congregation and especially to the most important and influential members of it. But this ceremony was difficult to keep up after the first years of enthusiasm had passed and fell into neglect. A curious feature of Huguenot discipline was that there was no religious service connected with funerals. All was to be done decently and in order; but no ministers were present nor were prayers said.

The tone of life was what in England would be called Puritan. Instrumental music was not allowed in church; dancing was sternly forbidden at weddings and was discountenanced at any time. A sobriety of dress and demeanour was recommended, though it was difficult to enforce it, especially among the aristocratic members of the congregation. The best known instance of this comes from the life of Madame du Plessis-Mornay. She has told us how the pastor Berault of Montauban refused to admit her to communion, unless she removed from her hair certain wires which she used to keep it in place. She protested that there was no passage in scripture or in any decision of a synod which forbade the use of wire in the hair. The pastor was not to be moved. She appealed to Henry of Navarre and we can well imagine the amusement which he would find in the case, which he would perhaps discuss with his mistress, Gabrielle D'Estrées. We do not know the result of the appeal. From the first there was some resistance to the " Puritan " discipline. The Sunday ought to have been kept free from ordinary pleasures and occupations, but it was never observed in France with the strictness that prevailed in England under the Puritan régime. The strong aristocratic element was always a difficulty. There were sometimes the same contests for precedences and positions in the Huguenot temples that there were in the salons of Versailles, and the orders of ministers and consistory can have had little weight in the 257 aristocratic congregations.

The Huguenots were drawn from every rank of society with the exception of the peasantry; of these there is little trace in their ranks in the more settled parts of France, but in the mountains of the Cevennes there were villages and districts where the whole population was in rebellion against Rome and her ways. Their separate religious ideas and organization date from long before the preaching of Calvin, but they had joined themselves to the Huguenot movement in spite of some differences of practice and belief. We shall have to take a careful note of them later, but for the present may pass from them.

We have insisted more than once on the large proportion of nobles who were to be found in the Huguenot ranks. They had been valuable defenders of the early movement and without them it would probably have been destroyed with fire and sword, but they were a dangerous element. There were many ardent believers among them; but political motives were strong if not predominant with them. To the Kings of France it must have seemed that the old feudal resistance to the Crown was being revived again under the cloak of religion. And the austerity of the Genevan rule was impossible of enforcement among them. The chief aristocratic families attached to the Huguenot movement may be noted. There was first the House of Bourbon, though by no means all its members took the same road in religious matters. No family had been so prominent in their ranks at first. The King and Queen of Navarre were striking examples of the different motives which led men to join themselves to the Huguenots ; King Antony, so light and self-seeking ; his wife Jeanne, devoted, ready to do and suffer all for the faith that she had adopted. There is more of Antony than of Jeanne in Henry of Navarre, though he had more strength of character than his father. Then there were the two Dukes of Condé, both Protectors of the Huguenots : the one was killed at Jarnac (1569), the other died in 1588. The family remained for two more generations loosely attached to the faith, but when the Crown had definitely triumphed in its struggle with its religious opponents they soon transferred their allegiance to the " royal " Church and probably found little searching of heart in making the change. We have seen the immense services which were rendered in the early days of the movement by the three Chatillon brothers of whom Coligny was Admiral of France and Odet was a Cardinal and Bishop of Beauvais ; it may be noted again that this family was closely related to the house of Montmorency, one of the most prominent of the noble houses of France. Next the capable and intriguing Bouillons deserve mention. In the next century the great Turenne was

75

a member of this family, one of the greatest soldiers in history, who, however, later transferred his loyalty to the Roman Catholic Church. Of Sully we have already spoken at some length. In the next generation his son-in-law, the Duke of Rohan, played a leading part in the last struggles of the party for independence. La Noue in the earlier period and Soubise in the early seventeenth century deserve a passing mention.

In thinking of the Huguenots we must not allow these aristocratic leaders to occupy our imagination to the exclusion of other and more important elements. The official representatives were of course the ministers. It was they who had to hold the churches together, often at the risk of much suffering and death. The French have always produced great preachers, and these Huguenot pastors had assuredly high talents. They expounded the scheme of salvation as contained in the *Institutes of the Christian Religion* ; they attacked the opposing views and defended their own in many a bitter controversy, and they maintained, not without much difficulty sometimes, the moral discipline that had been laid down at Geneva. Their great representative is Theodore de Beza, after Calvin the greatest Calvinist of the sixteenth century, unless the place be given to John Knox. He followed closely in the footsteps of Calvin. Like him he was at first intended for holy orders in the Catholic Church ; like him he transferred his attention to legal studies ; like him he withdrew from before the dangers that threatened in

France and found a home in Geneva. But he was often called thence to take a part in the religious drama that was being enacted in France. It was he who converted (for a time) Antony of Bourbon to the Calvinist faith. He played a leading part in the Colloquy at Poissy (1561) where he showed more inclination to conciliation with the Lutherans than would probably have been approved by Calvin, and declared that all were bound to obey the King absolutely " in everything except what concerned the service of God "—a large and significant reservation. We may often see him with the Huguenot armies, for he never lacked courage or enterprise. When Servetus was put to death for heresy in Geneva he defended the action of the magistrates, and he raged furiously against crosses and images. On Calvin's death he was made Head of the Company of Pastors at Geneva and was the recognized head of the Calvinists until his death in 1605. Like his master he was a considerable humanist as well as a theologian. In his catalogue of eighty-seven works are some on classical subjects and on the correct pronunciation of the French language. Along with him we may mention Chandieu, Pastor of the Church of Paris.

The real strength of the movement lay probably with the commercial and middle class. But it had more adherents among the professional classes than we should perhaps have expected. Lawyers and jurists were especially attracted to the party. Calvin and Beza passed through the study of the law to theology and their legal studies have left a strong mark on their theological system. Hotman and Languet, who wrote books of great importance for the development of the political thought of Europe, were Huguenots ; but of them we shall speak again shortly.

A number of important artists too were attached to the party with more or less of earnestness—but no one would join a body so despised and persecuted whose heart was not really won over by its tenets. There was Jean Cousin who has been called, with much exaggeration, the Michael Angelo of France. His works are rare, and many of them were on glass, but one painting still hangs in the gallery of the Louvre. There was Jean Goujon, a sculptor of really high rank, who worked for Catherine de Médicis and adorned the palace of the Tuileries with sculptures which are still to be seen there. His connexion with the royal family did not save him from falling a victim in the massacre of Saint Bartholomew's Day. Bernard Palissy (1510–90) is even more closely identified with the religious movement. He shared in the foundation of the Huguenot Church at Saintes and, despite the esteem in which his work in pottery was held among the rich and great, he was often in danger because of his faith. He died in the Bastille in 1590. He was certainly a great artist and there is hardly a more attractive character in France in the sixteenth century than this courageous, humorous, amusing Huguenot. His long struggles before he discovered the methods which were suitable for his art have something heroic about them. The products of his workshop are more and more valued by connoisseurs. His mind ranged widely over art and science and life. His name finds a place among those who groped towards a science of geology.

We have by no means exhausted the list of eminent Huguenots during the first century of the movement. There was Ambrose Paré, called by his Huguenot biographer " the father of modern surgery " and certainly one of the great contributors to the progress of surgery and medicine in his age. He served the state well at the siege of Metz and was highly valued by the royal household. It was it seems the favour of Charles IX that saved him from death on the day of the great massacre. There was Ramus (La Ramée), the humanist and philosopher. There was at the end of the century Casaubon, to whom Mark Pattison has devoted a charming volume of biography. He was perhaps the first latinist of his age and was called by Henry IV to the University of Paris. But his appointment there was unwelcome because of his faith, and he soon gladly accepted an invitation to England where he was admitted into the English Church and buried in Westminster Abbey. There was Clement Marot who must count as a Huguenot though his theological orthodoxy was at least doubtful. He declared " I am neither Lutheran nor Zwinglian and still less am I an Anabaptist. I am one who finds pleasure and duty in praising Christ and His mother so full of infinite grace." He translated the psalms and his very excellent version was used and constantly sung by the Huguenots and even by many who were not Huguenots. He was protected by the Court for a long time, but in the end had to flee to Geneva. There, however, he was not at his ease ; " for he could not bring his life into obedience to the Gospel." France was closed against him, but he retired to Italy and died at Turin. And no list of prominent Huguenots can omit Theodore Agrippa D'Aubigné. He was an excellent example of the aristocratic Huguenot full of undisciplined energy and daring, genuinely attached to his faith which he could not be induced to abandon ; but capable of committing in his private life much that ran counter to the discipline of Geneva. He was intimately associated with Henry of Navarre both before and after his acquisition of the throne. He had a vigorous and picturesque pen and wrote on many subjects, but he is remembered only by his Universal History, which is really French history, during the wars of religion, and by his more intimate Secret History.

The Huguenots then without question were no mere coterie. They were a section cut right through French society and were representative of nearly everything that was best in France.

What was the outlook of the Huguenots as a whole on political and social questions ? They were primarily a religious, not a political body ; but all religious movements have important reactions on every side of life and this is as true of Calvinism as of any other. They have even been claimed as " the liberals of the sixteenth century." How far is this claim true ?

Liberalism is a vague phrase and needs definition.

I take it as implying a claim for the individual to possess liberty in speech and organization ; freedom from arbitrary arrest ; freedom generally from the arbitrary action of the government and some share in the formation of government. The attitude of the Huguenots on these great questions was by no means consistent or uniform.

Calvin's position has often been analysed. He was full of respect for the State and for established authority ; for all to use his own words " which relates to civil justice and the regulation of external conduct " ; but his real interest lay with the other kind of government " that which is situated in the soul or the inner man and relates to eternal life." He denounced all ideas of anarchy as absurd and un-Christian and regarded all the historic forms of government as legitimate under different circumstances. Obedience to established governors was a duty " even though they perform none of the duties of their function." And men owed to their rulers not only obedience but also " the sentiments of affection and reverence." It is not for the private individual to criticize the action of the government. But where there are magistrates appointed for the protection of the people " such as the Ephors among the Spartans or the tribunes with the Romans or the Demarchs among the Athenians " it is their right and duty to protest against misgovernment. And the last clause of the Institute, though it follows inevitably from the central principle of Calvin's thought, opened a wider gate to rebellion than he probably realized.

" The Lord is the King of Kings. If they command anything against Him it ought not to have the least attention. We ought to obey God rather than men." The theocracy which he set up in Geneva gave little guidance to Calvinists elsewhere in solving the problem of how they should behave to a government hostile to their faith and discipline.

The most powerful and valuable contribution of Calvin to " liberalism " was not in theory but in the organization of his Church. For there self-government was everywhere to be found. Ministers and laymen sat and deliberated together. Consistories, provincial assemblies, national synods were an invaluable training in self-government, and the Kings of France were quite justified in regarding them as a dangerous rival to the government itself. The history of Scotland, where the General Assembly both claimed and for a time possessed power greater than that of Parliament or monarchy, is a sufficient proof of this. Within the Huguenot temples, in spite of the great influence possessed by the nobles, there was a measure of equality greater than was to be found elsewhere in the social life of France.

Huguenot opinion as expressed by their writers varied from time to time on the question of resistance to authority and the need for some sort of " parliamentary " institutions. Their relation to the government changed diametrically during the course of the religious wars. For at first the government was lukewarm in its protection and after the " Massacre " it was regarded as the cruellest and most treacherous of enemies. The

Huguenots then welcomed any political theory which would encourage resistance or give them the prospect of a different type of political organization. But later, first, the heir to the throne was their own leader ; and after the death of the Duke of Alençon he became King by right of heredity, and could only be kept from the throne by invoking against him some power in the people or in their represe-sentatives or in the Church to counteract his hereditary claim. Thus—as Montaigne noted with amusement—the combatants changed weapons. It was the Catholics of the League who appealed to States-General and some higher law than heredity, while the Huguenots were content to join with the Politiques in standing by the ancient traditions of the French monarchy and in repudiating all attempts to interfere with the action of hereditary claims.

August 24, 1572—the date of the Great Massacre —marked a dividing line in the attitude of the Huguenots to the government and to the question of the legitimacy of resistance to rulers. Pamphlets appeared which declared assassination to be admissible. The dethronement of the Valois was advocated, Catherine was now painted as the worst of criminals. Many of these utterances were merely the very natural cries of disappointment and anger ; but the situation left a permanent mark on the opinions of the most thoughtful writers of the party. There was published in 1573 at Geneva a book called *Franco-Gallia*, whose author was Francois Hotman, at one time Professor of Law in the University of Bourges. He examined the past history of France and found there free institutions of Germanic origin in conflict with the centralized monarchy which was derived from imperial Rome. He found throughout, what the modern historian has more difficulty in discovering, representative institutions which held the real sovereignty though the tyrant kings had managed to take it from them. Such representative bodies still had the right to elect or depose kings. Such teaching as this naturally supported the movement for the use of States-General, which was prominent during the last stage of the Religious Wars.

There were many other books produced on the Huguenot side by the grave dangers and difficulties which confronted them. Thus La Boétie's pamphlet, for it is little more, called *A Discourse on Voluntary Slavery*, though written many years previously now first saw the light. It is not the work of a Calvinist, but is a passionate call to the mass of the people to throw off the yoke of tyrants. It is the rhetorical work of a young man and must have been in harmony with much that was thought and felt on the Huguenot side. But the most serious book of the period on the Huguenot side is the " Defence against Tyrants " (*Vindiciæ contra tyrannos*) which appeared in 1579. Its authorship is still a matter of dispute. It has been attributed to Beza, to du Plessis-Mornay, and to a Huguenot called Languet.[1] It summed up the Huguenot

[1] Professor Barker has recently given what seem to me almost conclusive reasons for accepting the authorship of Languet.

84

views of government before the accession of Henry of Navarre to the throne changed their outlook, and if it had continued to represent the mind of the party would be sufficient proof that the Huguenots were indeed the liberals of Europe in the sixteenth century. Its central doctrine is contained in the following passage : " Princes are chosen by God but are established by the people. Private persons are inferior to princes ; but the whole people and those who represent them, being officials of the kingdom, are superior to the Prince. When a Prince is appointed there is made between him and the people a contract (*fœdus*) silent or expressed, natural or civil, to the effect that obedience should be rendered to him while he governs well and that all should serve one who serves the commonwealth. Now of this contract or pact the officials of the kingdom are the guardians and defenders. He who violates this contract treasonously and persistently shows himself in action a tyrant. The officials of the realm are thereupon bound by their office to judge him according to the laws, and, if other methods fail to restrain him, by violence. Let private persons or individuals never presume to draw the sword against proved tyrants, for they are appointed not by individuals but by the whole commonalty."

There may be nothing new in these doctrines, for we know now that liberalism has a long and even a medieval pedigree. They had soon to be omitted from the public utterances of the Huguenot party, for as we have said the championship of the

States-General and of the idea of establishing some popular control over Kings passed from the Huguenots to their opponents. But the ideas are found in the famous abjuration of William the Silent which was possibly composed by the same pen that wrote the Vindiciæ ; they were influential in translation with the English parliamentarians of the seventeenth century ; they are singularly close to the political philosophy of Locke. It is more important for our purpose to point out how strongly aristocratic are the deductions that the author draws from his central doctrine. It is not for the private man but only for the officials to take action against the wicked ruler. It is curious to note the list of officials which follows the passage above quoted. " The officials of the kingdom are of two kinds. Those who have undertaken the guardianship of the whole realm—as the Count of the Stable, Marshalls, Patricians, and Palatines— should with the connivance or assistance of the rest coerce the tyrant. Those who are the guardians of a part or of a district—such as Dukes, Marquises, Counts, Consuls, Mayors—can rightfully drive the tyranny and the tyrant from their district or city." We cannot doubt that the author is thinking of those nobles who controlled more than a quarter of the Huguenot congregations. The book seems to look to a provincial and federal rather than to a centralized parliamentary regime. The Condés, the Bouillons, the de la Noues of the party would be ready to welcome these ideas. But again we must repeat that it was the Catholic League rather than the Huguenots who made themselves the advocates of these ideas after 1584. The manifesto of the League declared that it desired to restore to the realm such rights and liberties as it possessed in the time of King Clovis, " or better if better could be found." In the end neither Huguenots nor Leaguers availed anything against the strong current in favour of national centralization in the hands of the King.

These ideas had no welcome naturally in the councils of King Henry IV. The *Mémoires* of Sully (the *économies royales* is their formal title) give us no formal treatise on politics and can only be accepted as authority on matters of fact with great caution. But they may be accepted as giving us the ideas current among the counsellors and companions of the King. Sully nowhere shows sympathy with any liberal ideas ; he shows not the least inclination to take the people into partnership in any form. He seems to have no sense of the importance of the method of election and does not distinguish between the elected States-General and the Notables who were merely the nominees of the Crown.

In conclusion the political theories of the Huguenots were strongly influenced by the changing needs of the time and by the strong aristocratic element in the movement. We can hardly exaggerate the influence of their aristocratic members on the history of the movement.

CHAPTER IV

RICHELIEU AND THE HUGUENOTS : THE SIEGE OF
ROCHELLE AND THE ANNIHILATION OF THE
POLITICAL POWER OF THE HUGUENOTS

THE first fifty years of the seventeenth century
were full of momentous events for the Huguenots.
They lost the footing of independence in relation
to the state which had been given them by the
Edict of Nantes ; they were decisively and finally
defeated by the government of France in a great
encounter ; and, though they retained their freedom of conscience and of worship and enjoyed a
position far better than that of religious dissidents
in most other countries, they depended for its
continuance on the ordinary action of the state
and the laws. If the state had been just and fair
to them, if the laws had maintained the conditions
that had been promised to them they would
have had little reason to complain. Nay, the
loss of their aristocratic protectors and allies
would have been a great gain. But the state
was not just to them, the laws proved a weak
defence for their rights and liberties. And so
there came the miserable tragedy of the Revocation of the Edict. We shall in this chapter

only follow their history as far as the death of Richelieu.

It is easy to see what were the forces—in the form of interests, passions or beliefs—which ruined the glorious work which had been accomplished when Henry IV signed the Edict at Nantes. There was first the widespread and almost universal acceptance of a view of religion which regarded heresy as a crime that ought to be punished and as a plague that ought to be stamped out before it infected others. The leaders of the Roman Church never moved from that position. Individual French Catholics saw their way to a wiser and more humane view, but from Rome there came nothing but denunciations of the view that heresy should be attacked only by humane and intellectual methods, nothing but enthusiasm as each step was taken which led to the final odious and suicidal crime. And next the idea of the unity of the state was against the Huguenots and more dangerous than the theological hatred which their worship aroused. Rapidly and almost universally the states of Europe were advancing towards concentration. This took the form in most countries of absorption of power in the hands of the King and of the bureaucracy which emanated at any rate in theory from him. Could political unity be maintained if there were not also unity in belief and worship and in the great principles on which life was based? The answer usually given was that religious unity was essential, that when freedom of worship was conceded it was a danger to the state, and that religious

89

organizations governing themselves independently of the state were a constant menace of civil war. There was much in the history of the Huguenot party in the last quarter of the sixteenth century and the first thirty years of the seventeenth which lent colour to this view. Richelieu struck his spectacular blow at Rochelle almost entirely in the interest of national unity and power ; he was hardly at all inspired by theological hatred.

While Henry IV lived the Huguenots had their grievances against him ; they thought that he leaned to the side of his new religious associates and against his old comrades. But they were sure he would not entirely abandon them. Just at the end of his reign the European situation grew more favourable to them. Henry watched Germany with close observation. He feared German unity as all French statesmen have always feared it ; and he feared anything that seemed likely to lead to an increase of the power of the Austrian house. A disputed succession in the Duchies of Juliers and Cleves seemed likely to lead to such an increase. He prepared to throw the armed strength of France into the contest in alliance with the Protestant powers of Europe. Such action would probably have led to a strengthening of the position of the Huguenots in France. The dagger of a Catholic fanatic ended all that in 1610. His eldest child was only nine years old. The regency came inevitably into the hands of his widow, Marie de Medicis, strongly Catholic and Spanish in her sympathies. The era of civil wars seemed likely to recommence and fighting did actually break out. What part would the Huguenots take ?

Sully was dismissed. The politician and statesman in him had always taken precedence of the Huguenot ; but his influence with the King was a valuable protection to the party. He protested against his dismissal and said that it contravened the Edict of Nantes, but his time of power was irrevocably over. His son-in-law Henry, Duke of Rohan, became one of the leading figures among the Huguenots. He was a fiery ambitious young man with none of the shrewdness and *savoir-faire* that had always distinguished his father-in-law, but his devotion to the Calvinist faith was sincere. The Huguenots received a further organization. " Circles " were established intermediate between the General and the Provincial Assemblies ; the idea and the name was clearly taken from Germany and was disquieting to the government. In 1612 war seemed imminent. The Huguenots gave all their confidence to the impetuous Rohan. In an Assembly held at Saumur he attacked vehemently the Catholic and Spanish policy of the Queen Regent and was quite clearly ready to raise the standard of rebellion at La Rochelle. More pacific counsels prevailed. Bouillon, who was a strong opponent of Rohan, and du Plessis-Mornay threw their long experience and the influence which belonged to their high rank against war. The government made concessions ; Rohan's position as Protector of the Huguenots was recognized : financial concessions were made to the ministers and the danger of war passed.

The Huguenot party under their aristocratic leaders had nearly precipitated a war. Richelieu was beginning to follow public affairs with keen interest, and the object lesson would not be lost on him.

The danger came again in an acute form in 1615. The Duke of Condé, a Prince of the blood and the grandson of that Duke of Condé who had been Protector of the Huguenots at the outbreak of the civil wars, gave voice to the discontents of the aristocracy and to a less degree of the people of France. He was not a Huguenot, but he made himself the spokesman of their party, and denounced the government for its attitude to them. He specially noted that books, circulated with the approval of the government, denounced liberty of conscience as the cause of the troubles of France. There was actual civil war and the Protestants took the lead in resistance. Many abstained, but in three provinces—Languedoc, Guienne, and Poitou— the Huguenots mobilized at the order of the Assembly which was held at Nîmes. The Duke of Rohan, the official Protector of the Huguenots, took up arms, but there were some Huguenot nobles who declared themselves ready to support the government ; and the trouble was soon settled by concessions on the side of the government. In the Treaty of Loudun (May 1616), the Huguenots gained important points, especially an increase in the pay which the government gave to the ministers and the garrisons of the Huguenots. They were also to be permitted to hold their garrison towns for another six years. They asked that the government would omit the word " Prétendue " from their official title which was " La religion prétendue réformée " (the so-called Reformed Religion), but this was not conceded.

The European world has never been more confused or difficult to understand than it was at the beginning of the seventeenth century. In Germany events were moving rapidly forward to the Thirty Years' War. For on the one side the impetus of the Protestant movement seemed to have spent itself. The Lutheran princes were ready to make their peace with the Empire, and what energy there was in the Protestant camp was to be found chiefly among the Calvinists. And, while German Protestantism flagged, the forces of the Counter Reformation, represented especially by the Jesuits, were full of ardour and of hope. It seemed possible that Protestantism might be destroyed in its first home. Such a prospect would have had nothing in itself unwelcome to the rulers of France. But there were military and political possibilities as well as religious in the German fermentation. The Hapsburg rulers saw a chance of turning their almost nominal imperial power into something real and effective. It was the last time that fortune dangled that tempting bait before them. It seemed that they might hope to overthrow the independent power of the Princes and to rule in Germany as the Kings of France or of Spain or of England ruled in their respective countries. If the Emperors won this dazzling prize the work of Bismarck would be anticipated and France would have to face a united Germany across the Rhine. This was the nightmare that continually pressed on the imagination of French statesmen and that was the constant preoccupation of Richelieu and Mazarin. And it was not Germany alone that was in confusion. The clash between Parliament and Crown had begun in England. James I had tried to reverse Elizabeth's policy of friendliness with France in favour of a Spanish alliance. The plan was clumsily contrived and had failed grotesquely. Its failure led to a sudden return to friendly relations with France and these were shortly cemented by the marriage of the Prince, who would soon be King Charles I, with Henrietta Maria, the daughter of Henry IV of France. A good understanding between France and England was always favourable to the Huguenots, but the good prospect was soon darkened as we shall shortly see. We must not extend our view of European politics more widely. The waters seemed everywhere in violent commotion without showing anywhere a decided set of the tide in any direction.

The outlook in France was not much plainer. Some thought that a new era of civil wars was preparing ; that England would use the civil and religious commotions of France in order to regain a hold on the country, and that the great nobles in alliance with Protestant separatism might do for France much what similar forces had done for Germany.

Then Richelieu came. He was made Bishop of

Luçon in 1607 and received the Cardinal's hat in 1622. But, Bishop and Cardinal though he was, the chief impulse of his whole career is political and national. His life and work are full of strange paradoxes. This weak ecclesiastic, who was sometimes prostrated by headaches which prevented him even at most critical moments from attending to business, dominated Europe at a time when force and violence seemed to decide everything. This Cardinal of the Church of Rome crossed the most cherished designs of the Pope and his advisers at every turn and saved the Protestants of Germany in the hour of their greatest need. This great servant of the Crown, who raised the French monarchy to the highest pinnacle of power in Europe, was at constant feud with most of the members of the royal family—the King's mother and wife and brother—and was by no means always loyally supported even by the King himself.

But there is no difficulty in solving the riddle of his life. In his *Testament Politique* he has stated his aims with a clearness and definiteness unexampled in the utterance of any great statesman. He made for a single goal and that goal was the strength and unity of France. His attitude to the King was very different from that of the cavaliers of England, but he saw in the monarchy the agency through which his object could alone be attained ; and neglecting or destroying all rival institutions, discarding the States-General, coercing the legal corporations, overriding the free towns, he built up the centralized monarchy into an efficient machine which was the envy and admiration of all the crowned heads of Europe.

How would the Huguenots fare when the dexterous fingers of Richelieu controlled the strings of French diplomacy and statecraft? Theological antipathies had little weight with him. They called him in Rome "atheist" and the Pope of the Huguenots. But a million and a quarter of Frenchmen holding meetings of their own, controlling a considerable portion of the French army, strongly entrenched in over a hundred strong places in France, and intimately associated with some of the great aristocratic families of the country—here was a force that was bound to attract the attention and the alarm of a statesman whose passion was for unity and uniformity.

Let us listen to two paragraphs from the opening chapter of his *Testament Politique* in which he sets down the outlines of his policy and his mature judgment on public affairs. "When your Majesty decided to give me a place in your councils and a great part in your confidence for the direction of public business I can say with truth that the Huguenots divided the state with you ; that the Nobles acted as though they were not subjects ; and that the most powerful Governors of Provinces seemed to be sovereigns within the sphere of their duties. . . . I promised your Majesty to employ all my energy and all the authority that it pleased you to give me in order to ruin the Huguenot party, to bring down the pride of the Nobles, to reduce your subjects to their duties and to raise your name among foreign nations to the place which it ought to hold."

These words ring like a declaration of war. We will try to see the last great struggle of the Huguenots from their own point of view. But before we pass over to their side it is well to recognize that there was much in the position that they had won which could not be brought into a harmony with the life of the modern state. What would one of the English Tudor monarchs have said if he had been asked to allow the Roman Catholics or the Calvinists of England such privileges as the Huguenots held in France ? Very slowly has it been discovered that the unity of the state is not necessarily broken up by freedom of association, but no modern state could tolerate the military privileges which were allowed to the Huguenots by the great Edict. Recent events in Italy, Germany, Russia and elsewhere show how far many great states of to-day are from admitting freedom of thought, speech, and organization. The spirit of Mussolini, Hitler, and the Russian Soviets would be more hostile to the Huguenot position than Richelieu himself.

It is well to mark the stages by which Richelieu climbed to almost absolute power in France. It was through the favour of Marie de Médicis, the Queen Mother, that he first gained access to the Council of the King in November 1616. Events at Court, which we must not try to disentangle here, led to his speedy dismissal and he did not enter the royal Council again until 1624. It was in August of that year that he became Chief of the

Council and it is then that his real reign began. But he was an important influence before that. He was chosen in 1620 to carry out an important negotiation between the King and his mother, and from that time onwards was in close touch with public affairs, though he did not control the policy of France until 1624.

It is easy to understand the aims and the hopes of the royal and Catholic party in France. The thoughts of the Huguenot party are not so clear. In truth it was rapidly ceasing to be one party and was torn by irreconcilable divisions. The nobles were drawing away from it, and their control of its councils was by no means so complete as it had been. Many passed over to the side of the King and were prepared to pass over to the side of the Pope. Bouillon was the most distinguished nobleman in the party, and he was prepared to play a great diplomatic game, linking up the Protestants of France with the schemes of the Protestant powers of Europe in the struggle against the Catholic Reaction ; but he would not work with the men who were gaining control of the councils of the Huguenots at this time. Lesdiguières, du Plessis-Mornay, the aged Sully shared his views. But there was one nobleman who rejected all thought of weakness or accommodation and that was the Duke of Rohan, of whom we have already spoken. A great French historian [1] has drawn an admirable portrait of him. " Rohan," he writes, " is a hero excellently representative of his party. He pos-

[1] Hanotaux, in his *Cardinal de Richelieu*, II, 2.

sessed in the highest degree all the qualities and virtues of French Protestantism ; purity of morals, tenacity of purpose, sobriety of judgment and obstinacy. . . . He spoke little, but when he did it was with a concentration of passion ; he wrote much and well. He was always self-controlled and knew how to yield when the occasion called for it, and for all his reserve he loved applause and popularity. He would have been the Cæsar of the Protestant party if we could imagine Cæsar a Huguenot." He has written memoirs which tell us much that is interesting, but omit also very much that we should like to know. He expresses a preference for daring measures over the counsels of timidity ; he is full of criticism and of jealous suspicion against the other Huguenot leaders ; and above all he very rarely speaks of religion. In his speeches, which are full of power, he says that he " will always support the cause of God and will think it an honour to suffer for His name." But in the *Mémoires* he speaks only of personal and political motives. There may have been in him something of Cæsar—though I think not much— but there was little of Cromwell.

Influence in the Huguenot party was passing away from the nobles and was being claimed by the more popular elements of the party in a way which finds its parallels both in the history of the English Puritans and the Scotch Presbyterians. Here the ministers had great influence. As we read of some of them we are reminded of Obadiah Walker at the siege of Londonderry, or of the Scotch ministers who controlled the action of the Scotch armies when they were fighting against Cromwell or Claverhouse. The Huguenots advocated a large measure of independence for the cities where they were strong ; they spoke of some representative body of the Protestants of the whole realm which should be for France what the States of Holland were for the Dutch. The whole of the Protestants of France were by no means carried away by these ideas ; there was conflict between districts as well as between classes within the Huguenot body. But when Richelieu said that they aimed at constituting " a state within a state " he was justified by the facts.

During the days when Richelieu was feeling his way to power there had broken out a new Huguenot war which as it leads up to the Siege of Rochelle and the Peace of Alais deserves to be noted in its main features.

It had its origin in Béarn which, closely united with Navarre, had given to Henry IV his first royal title. Its government had been keenly and exclusively Protestant. It was a state independent of France, though the King of France was King also of Navarre and Béarn, and the laws of France did not apply to it. Its position—to compare a small state to a much larger one—was the same as that of Scotland after King James VI of Scotland had become King James I of England. When Henry abjured Protestantism he had reintroduced Catholic worship into Béarn, from which it had been banished for many years, and where there was a large Catholic population; 4 6 6 3 7 and he promised to restore to the Catholic Church the property that had once been in their hands. The question was a difficult one and Henry had avoided it ; but his successor took it up.

It was not merely a question of money, for the Huguenot ministers would certainly be otherwise provided for ; but it was a blow against the Huguenot position in the dominions of Louis XIII which might be followed by others. The Huguenots of Béarn appealed to the Huguenots of France for support and the General Assembly meeting at Loudun decided to support them. Their decision was natural and generous, but it was an interference in the relations of the Crown of France with a foreign power—for Béarn, as we have seen, was independent—and it increased the hostility of the Crown to the privileges of the Huguenots. Events moved slowly, but in 1617 the King issued a definite order restoring to the Catholic Bishops the property that had belonged to them in Béarn. The little state prepared to resist and again asked for the support of the Huguenots of France. In 1619 the Protestant Assembly was moved to La Rochelle where it sat for the future. Violent counsels prevailed. Lescun, a lawyer, was the chief influence ; the ministers took his side in advocating resistance at all cost ; many of the nobles fell away, but Rohan stood firmly with them. The atmosphere at La Rochelle was revolutionary in character and the mass of the people were, it would seem, ready to welcome the hopeless struggle.

The struggle in Béarn was soon over. The young King was excited by this his first military experience. Béarn was occupied without much difficulty. Béarn and Navarre were now definitely and finally united to the Crown of France. The Catholic Bishops received back their property. No effective help had come from the French Huguenots. But the part they had taken or had wished to take could hardly be overlooked by the French government.

The war that followed was not conducted with more energy or success than those which had been waged against the same enemies by Catherine de Médicis and her children. There was no hint of the efficiency and determination which was soon to characterize the policy of France when once Richelieu, who now watched critically the conduct of affairs from the side of the Queen Mother, at last arrived at power. The royal forces were overwhelmingly strong in the field. The guarantee towns made little resistance and most of them were surrendered by their commanders into the hands of the Crown. Saumur was taken. Saint-Jean-d'Angely was defended for a time by Soubise, the gallant and headstrong brother of Rohan, but was forced to yield. The Constable Luynes, the favourite of the King and his first Minister, believed himself sure of a great triumph. But then there came disappointment. Luynes took the King to superintend the siege of the strong city of Montauban. He believed that the siege would be a short one ; he had intelligence with agents within the city who had promised to betray it to him. But all his calculations proved false. His agents were discovered and executed. The population resisted with a stubbornness that was strengthened by religious zeal. The Duke of Rohan commanded a force outside of the city and threatened the communications of the royal army. Worst of all, plague broke out in the ranks of the royal army. The siege had to be abandoned.

The war went on yet a while. Condé directed the military operations for the Crown. Soubise was defeated with heavy loss. Many of the Huguenot nobility—Sully, La Force, Chatillon—withdrew from the contest. No further attempt was made on Montauban, but Condé led the royal army to lay siege to Montpellier. But here the story of the siege of Montauban was repeated. Rohan remained outside and harried the army of Condé with great courage and much success. Attacks on the walls were repulsed with much loss. Most important of all, the civil war was weakening the action of France in foreign affairs. The relation between the Huguenots and the general European contest was the essential feature of the situation as it presented itself to Richelieu and all who thought like him. There seemed a great likelihood that the schemes of Austria and Spain would be successful ; that the Hapsburg House would overthrow its enemies in Germany and would reduce Protestantism to a quite subordinate position and vastly increase the strength of the Empire ; that Spain would be able to master the important corridor of the Valtelline in upper Italy and thus secure a land passage for her troops from Italy to the Low Countries. If these things happened, France would feel herself encircled and strangled. Richelieu wished to bring the civil struggle to an end and throw all the strength of France into the European struggle. He was not yet master of France, but his ideas triumphed when the King decided to abandon the siege of Montpellier and make peace with the Huguenots. They had been throughout in communication with Spain and England. Their necessity forced them to ask the help of foreign powers; but it was in the end their undoing. Now from England Rohan received advice to conclude peace and thus there came the Peace of Montpellier. The Edict of Nantes was confirmed; but the position of the Huguenots had much deteriorated. The only strong places that they now held were La Rochelle and Montauban. The holding of political assemblies such as those which from La Rochelle had directed the course of this war was expressly forbidden. When next the government of France made war against the Huguenots the dice would be heavily loaded against them.

The Duke of Rohan was blamed by the fiercer spirits of his party for having made or consented to the peace. He defended himself in a speech which is printed in his *Mémoires* by showing how little support he had received from the nobles of the party and even from other Huguenot cities and congregations and by detailing the extremities to which the garrison of Montpellier was reduced.

Before we come to the next scene in the Huguenot drama it is well to note how closely connected Rohan had been all along with foreign powers and especially with England. The English ambassador had sent his secretary to him at Montauban and the King of England had written to him at Montpellier " advising me above all things to make peace and to place all my trust in the word of my King since it was impossible for any help to come from England."

The Peace was of short duration. It makes indeed these events clearer if we recognize that there was no peace and could be none. The position of the Huguenots accorded to them by the Edict of Nantes and the claims they founded on it could not be accepted by the French Government except as temporary measure. They were an armed force encamped in France in league with foreign powers. Their character excites our admiration ; they contained moral and intellectual elements that France could ill afford to lose ; they were treated, especially by Louis XIV, with the greatest injustice and cruelty. But if France was to be united and strong it must be made impossible for a Rohan to hold the field with a force of his own against the armies of France and for La Rochelle to treat with the Kings of France as an independent power.

Fighting began again in January 1625. Rohan complained that the Edict of Nantes was being broken. The people of La Rochelle complained of the Fort Saint-Louis which had been built so as to command the entrance to the harbour. Rohan's madcap brother Soubise precipitated war by seizing the Île de Ré which lies some ten miles from the mouth of the harbour. This was by no means the end of his exploits. He seized seven royal ships that were in the River Blavet in Brittany. He was then shut up in the harbour that he had seized—and his capture seemed certain. But with great daring he cut the boom that had been thrown across the harbour mouth and was soon at sea again. This time he laid hands on the Isle of Oléron lying some twenty-five miles to the south of La Rochelle. Rohan recounts these exploits in his memoirs with an admiration and an enthusiasm which the reader can easily share. But if he was allowed to go on unchecked there was an end of France as a European power. Rohan at the same time collected forces in Languedoc and prepared for war on a great scale.

It was certainly not beyond the power of France to crush out the military power of the Huguenots. Richelieu appreciated to the full the danger that was implied in their action. An attack on them would have been welcomed by nearly every element at Court. And yet he determined to make peace with them. His eyes were fixed on the European situation. He wanted above all things to throw the might of a united France across the designs of Spain and Austria, and that was impossible while the Huguenots were in a state of civil war. He determined to bring the war to an end by a compromise and carried out his purpose in the face of great difficulties. Once, when peace seemed assured, the royal garrison of Fort Saint-Louis suddenly attacked the people of La Rochelle and killed many of them. But Richelieu persisted, and he was supported by the good offices of the English and Dutch. It was doubtless ignominious to accept the help of foreigners in a domestic settlement, but he wished at all costs to remove the Huguenot difficulty, and peace was signed in February 1626. It was almost a treaty between two equal powers. The people of La Rochelle promised to keep no armed vessels and in their trade to observe the ordinary practices of the rest of France. They had asked for the destruction of the menacing Fort Saint-Louis, but this the King would not grant. Only in the sixth article he promised that the garrisons of the fort and also of the islands of Ré and Oléron should be kept in good order and not allowed to interfere with the freedom and safety of the commerce of the city. There was little chance of stability for such an arrangement.

There was no fighting for rather more than a year. Then came the last and decisive contest, and the political and military power of the Huguenots foundered after a heroic struggle that has not ceased to attract the admiration of posterity.

The principle of Richelieu's treatment of the Huguenots up to this time is plain. He wanted to be free from civil war in order to devote all the strength of France to the foreign struggle. It had always been difficult to keep foreign and domestic difficulties separate. But now they became intimately and obviously identified. A war with England led to the rebellion of the Huguenots. Richelieu saw that the only way to be free of the religious difficulty was to crush the Huguenots, and he carried through his purpose with that unflinching energy which is characteristic of him.

The causes of the English war must not detain us long. King James I's effort to make an alliance with Spain had failed utterly. He had swung round for a time to the traditional policy of an *entente* with France, and the *entente* was to be sealed by a marriage. It was in appearance very much like the projects of the years 1570–2 when a marriage between Queen Elizabeth and the French King's brother was sought in order to ensure the permanence of the Anglo-French alliance. This time the marriage was carried through ; Henrietta Maria, the daughter of Henry of Navarre and the sister of the reigning Louis XIII, became the wife of Prince Charles who would soon succeed to the English throne as Charles I. But hardly was the marriage concluded when troubles began to arise. The ostensible cause of these was the arrangements made for the young Queen's religious life in England. Protestant opinion was indignant at the sight of the array of priests—accompanied by a Bishop—who came over with Henrietta Maria, and she and her religious advisers were certainly unwise in the openness with which they paraded their religious observances and hopes. Most of the Queen's clerical attendants were dismissed in spite of protests from France. There ran too through all these serious complications a famous personal intrigue. The Duke of Buckingham during his visit to France with Prince Charles had seen the Queen Mother. He fancied himself in love with her and he fancied—with less foundation —that his love was returned. He was anxious to support any scheme which would bring him back again to France even in the capacity of an invader. But more important than this personal intrigue, more important probably even than the religious difficulties of the French princess, were the naval and commercial rivalries of the two countries. Richelieu desired to make France a strong naval power. He saw with a clearness unusual in that age the all-importance of maritime power and was determined to challenge the power of Holland and England by sea as well as on land. The government, and still more the commercial classes, in England were not slow to feel the threat, and attacks on French commercial vessels hardly ceased. Vessels were seized at Dover under the eyes of a French ambassador. Many similar outrages were reported from various parts of the Channel.

Under the influence of these different motives England entered on aggressive war. The motive of religion was put forward. England had negotiated the late peace between the Huguenots and the government and claimed the right to protest against its infraction. Grandiose plans for the invasion of France were talked of. One expedition was to land near Bordeaux ; another was to land in Normandy ; a third was to join itself to the

Huguenots at La Rochelle. Rohan was approached and promised to do what he could to raise the Protestant south as soon as he knew that the English had actually landed in France.

Of the three expeditions projected the expedition to La Rochelle was the only one to materialize. But before we follow the fortunes of the tragic struggle we must notice the situation of La Rochelle. The harbour was for the vessels of those days a fine one. But in front of the estuary that led up to the city there lay two islands. The island of Ré was some ten miles to the north-west ; the larger isle of Oléron was about twice as far off to the south-west. An enemy in possession of either island could constantly threaten and injure the trade of the city. Ré was of the greater military importance, but Oléron was much more fertile and its population —Rohan tells us—was almost entirely Protestant. The defences of La Rochelle itself were very strong. Marshes kept off the approach of an enemy on the east and south. The walls were strong and recently improved. Their strength is proved by the fact that the French army made no attempt to take the city except by famine. On the north side of the estuary and near its mouth the King had constructed the fort of Saint-Louis. It was the " eyesore " of La Rochelle. The citizens had constantly petitioned to have it removed but in vain. The population of the city was large and reached something like 25,000. The courage of the people was soon to be proved by their memorable defence of their city.

What was the position of the city internally ? It had been the chief stronghold of the Huguenots since 1568, and after the great massacre the remnant of the party had found refuge behind its walls. It had then stood a siege which had perhaps been the salvation of the cause. A little earlier the Queen of Navarre had brought her son Henry there to share the lot of her co-religionists. Of late years the Council of the Huguenots had sat permanently there, though there were many of the party, especially in the south-east, who did not admit the right of the Rochellois to decide the policy for the whole body. The temper of the city was different from what was to be found in the more aristocratic atmosphere of Languedoc and Provence. The middle class had the chief influence and with them were associated the ministers. But there was no decided anti-aristocratic movement. Soubise was often there and exercised great influence. Rohan thought it wisest, in the interest of the defence of the city, to keep the war alight in the south-east, but his mother and sister were from the first within the walls. They felt themselves safer there than elsewhere.

The government of the city was that of many other communes of France at this time. It was in the hands of a mayor, twenty-four aldermen and seventy-four *pairs* or councillors. The aldermen were in effect hereditary and enjoyed high privileges. The mayor was chosen by the King out of a list of three submitted to him by the council. Twelve of the aldermen in rotation formed an inner council along with the mayor. These acted as a tribunal, but they were also the real executive government of the city. Under the stress of the siege the government became, as was natural, more centralized. The celebrated mayor, Guiton, already well known for his daring as a sailor and corsair, exercised a sort of dictatorship during the siege. There was also the usual religious organization for the city in the form of a consistory. There was some opposition to the Huguenots but not much. There was a court called the *présidial* appointed by the King which of course resisted the policy of rebellion, and there were elements in the population which would have liked to avoid the sufferings which the siege was certain to entail whatever its issue. But when once the fighting had begun all opposition was crushed and the city seemed unanimous in its desperate resistance.

The story of the siege comes to us mainly from the pens of the enemies of the Huguenots. It is easy to see the life of the great camp which Richelieu established for the blockade of the city. We can see him in half-clerical, half-military dress, going his rounds and maintaining discipline with the help of other episcopal and monastic chiefs. We can see the occasional conversions of prominent Huguenots which were celebrated in the camp, for the whole movement had in the eyes of many something of the character of a crusade. It was perhaps the most critical moment in the career of the Cardinal-Minister, for there were many who desired his overthrow so eagerly that they would

have welcomed the failure of the siege as a means
to his fall. In the *Mémoires* which pass under his
name, and which certainly represent his own views,
he has given us a most interesting and valuable
though by no means always a wholly truthful
account of the events of the time, and half a dozen
other memoir writers fill the gaps which are left
by his narrative. But it is hard to penetrate within
the walls of the city. The Duke of Rohan, the head
of the Huguenot party, has written memoirs and his
mother and sister were among the besieged, but his
account of the events of the siege is singularly
jejune. Nor do we get the information that we
desire from any other source. We see the Mayor
Guiton threatening with his dagger any who dared
to speak of surrender even when famine had begun
to press hard on the city. We can see the watchers
straining their eyes day and night for some sign of
the arrival of the English fleet. We can see the
streets almost blocked with the dead when at last
surrender became inevitable. But most of the
movements within the city are unknown to us. We
cannot hear the debates in the council chamber or
—what would be very interesting—the sermons
preached in the Temple. The city suffered from
the extremity of famine, as Jerusalem and Carthage
and many another city in history have suffered, but
we have no pictures of the sufferings by an eye-
witness.

The struggle was far more a war between France
and England than between the French Government
and the rebellious Protestants. Rohan was engaged

in many adventures in Provence and Languedoc and the adjacent countries and he acquitted himself with vigour and daring ; for it is unworthy of Richelieu to malign him and even to throw doubt on his courage. But he made no effort to relieve La Rochelle and his actions had no real influence on the course of the siege nor on the ultimate fate of the Huguenots. And at La Rochelle itself there was not much fighting, though there was much suffering. There was one question on which all depended. Could the English expeditionary force make a successful landing ? Could they get into touch with the Rochellois. If they could, the Huguenots would not be crushed, and a patched peace of some sort would lead to the overthrow of Richelieu. But the English had not the energy or the strength necessary for the enterprise ; and their failure left the Huguenots of La Rochelle and France at the mercy of the Cardinal.

The Duke of Buckingham has been bitterly blamed for his conduct of the expedition by all parties. If he had made straight for La Rochelle he would have entered without much difficulty ; if he thought it best to seize one of the outlying islands it would have been better to seize Oléron than Ré ; when he had landed at Ré he might have captured the fort and island if he had pressed on rapidly ;—these are the charges that are made against him. Toiras, who was in command of the royal fortress at Saint-Martin on the island, has also incurred Richelieu's very sharp censures, for not having provided the fortress with a sufficiency of men and munitions and provisions.

The landing was effected in July 1626 after " a fortunate and glorious action," but nothing was won while the fort of Saint-Martin held out. It was hard pressed and provisions were extremely scarce, but Richelieu devoted all his energies to throwing in supplies and was successful ; he speaks with a soldier's admiration of the daring of his agents by whom this was accomplished. Even so Toiras was in the greatest distress and talked seriously of surrender when an expedition which had been collected at Oléron by the Bishop of Mende—one of the many churchmen who gave Richelieu most unchurchmanlike services—attacked the harbour with success. Buckingham drew off his forces with very heavy loss and went back to England. He as well as Richelieu had had his whole career at stake. English history might have taken a different turn if he had come back in triumph.

In La Rochelle there had been much hesitation about joining openly with " the old enemy." They held in characteristic fashion a public fast just when Buckingham was landing in Ré. The King of England sent them a letter signed by his own hand, in which he promised to bear all the expense of the expedition and not to insist on their repudiating their loyalty to their own King. They had already admitted an English envoy—he had come into the city arm in arm with Soubise and the mother of the Duke of Rohan—and the alliance of the city with the English was certain.

The fighting on the island of Ré had been followed of course with tense anxiety. When Buckingham retired to England it was certain that the city would incur the whole force of the Cardinal's hostility. The English leader had promised to return soon with a stronger force and urged the Huguenots to hold out at all costs until he returned.

Richelieu made no attempt to capture the city by assault. Few fortresses were so taken in the seventeenth century, for the methods of defence were superior to those of attack. But he drew a line of trenches and towers right round the city leaving only the estuary by which La Rochelle could communicate with the outside world. But if that gap remained open the blockade was useless, for through that the besieged could communicate with England and introduce food and reinforcements. It was clear that the gap must be closed. The approach from the sea must be barred as it had been when Antwerp fell into the hands of the Spaniards. It would be no easy task even for modern engineering. The Atlantic tide poured up the estuary and would make short work of any wall of masonry that tried to keep it out. But the tide might be guided and narrowed if not entirely excluded, and the passage might be blocked by dykes, booms, sunken vessels and all the resources of the age. It was an Italian engineer whom the French call Pompée Targon, who was chiefly answerable for the works, though he was much assisted by Frenchmen. A breakwater of masonry was pushed from either side of the channel leaving a broad tideway in the middle. This was guarded by every sort of appliance, especially by French ships within the breakwater and sunken vessels outside. There was too a stockade of piles driven into the bed of the river at low tide. By this means La Rochelle was to be locked up. Could the English get in before the lock was completed or could they break it when it was finished ? The whole issue lay in the answer to this question. The Rochellois and the English both believed the task was possible and not very difficult. It was perhaps impossible ; it was at any rate not achieved ; and the failure carried with it one of the great tragedies of history.

Before the works were completed Lord Denbigh arrived with an English fleet of sixty sail. He managed to get a message to the city saying that the citizens must clear the passage for him to sail in. It was impossible for them to do so. After a little rather aimless bombardment of the breakwater Lord Denbigh made no further attempt at the relief of the city but sailed back to England. The Huguenots believed themselves betrayed. It seems impossible to acquit Lord Denbigh of lukewarmness in the affair.

When the English fleet sailed off on May 19, 1628, the Rochellois must have felt that their chances of success were small. But they faced their fate with a courage and determination which would have been impossible without the help of their religious enthusiasm. The municipal government was overridden by the more centralized form of control that the situation demanded. A new council of war was instituted. It consisted of nineteen members ; but the guiding spirit was the mayor, Jean Guiton, the almost legendary hero of the siege. He had been elected—unwillingly it is said—on April 30, 1628. He laid his dagger on the table and said that he would stab anyone who spoke of surrender and asked to be so treated if the word came from his own lips. "We must frighten spies and traitors," he said, and he ruled by terror in a way that reminds us of the leaders of the Committee of Public Safety in 1793. There were, of course, some in the city who would have liked to purchase life by the acceptance of reasonable terms, but they were hunted down, and some were executed. After that the siege went on to its end without any audible differences among the citizens in spite of the constantly increasing sufferings. When in August a councillor said that it would be best to treat while yet there was some possibility of resistance, Guiton went up to him and struck him. "I will tell you," he said on another occasion, "what will be the pity of the enemy. Our men will be hanged and our women will be handed over to the soldiery. While there are enough of us left to shut the gates I will never consent that they should be opened." There were occasional sorties ; before the completion of the dyke occasional vessels slipped through and some brought a little food back into the city. But these incidents could not change the situation. The army of Richelieu—25,000 strong, while the Rochellois had diminished to not half that number—remained entrenched round the city. They were well paid, well fed and carefully controlled. Their losses from the enemy were very small, but at one time the marsh fever caused many deaths and placed a very large number *hors de combat*. The soldiers in a great military undertaking can rarely have had so easy a life as the royal army before La Rochelle.

The breakwater and works were finished ; the trap was closed ; that was the supreme fact. Would the English be able to open it ? That was the supreme question.

Buckingham had fully intended himself to conduct an expedition and had been talking to Soubise of his plans a few minutes before he was murdered by Felton. His death did not cause the expedition to be abandoned, for the Parliament had voted supplies and the honour of England was clearly involved. The fleet sailed under Lord Lindsay and appeared before La Rochelle on September 18, 1628. The attack this time was pressed with more vigour. Explosive machines were sent against the stockade but did little damage. There was heavy cannonading, but at too great a distance to be effective. The English fleet withdrew and there was no probability that another attempt would be made with better fortune. It did not return to England but remained in the neighbourhood to negotiate terms for the remnant that remained in La Rochelle.

Even Guiton saw now that the gates must be opened. The whole population was dying of starvation in no metaphorical sense. Non-combatants had been driven from the city, but they had not been allowed to pass through the encircling lines and returned to intensify the starvation of the garrison. There was no food and none could be procured. The dead lay in the streets and the living were too few and too weak to bury them. Cannibalism was reported. The details of any blockade pushed to its utmost extremity have a horrible uniformity. No besieged city—not even Jerusalem or Carthage—has suffered with more constancy the pressure of famine than La Rochelle did. A little more delay and Richelieu would have triumphed over a city of the dead. Guiton had consented to negotiate just before the arrival of Lord Lindsay's expedition. That expedition had changed for a moment despair into exultant hope ; but its departure brought despair back again.

Richelieu refused to admit the mediation of the King of England. The account must be settled between the King of France and his subjects now once for all. Even at the last the Rochellois showed the courage that was in them. Let us hear Richelieu. " The audacity which always goes with rebellion was so deeply implanted in the minds of these wretches that, though they were no more than the shadows of living men and the only life which was left to them lay in the mercy of the King of which they were unworthy, they proposed to the cardinal to make a general treaty in the name of the party and claimed the continuation of their ancient privileges, franchises and immunities. . . . The Cardinal laughed at their impudence and told them that they must hope for nothing else but pardon and that they did not deserve even that." On October 28 the treaty " or rather the grant of terms " was signed by which the King gave life and possession of their property to all who were in the city and the free exercise of the " so-called Reformed religion ". On October 30 the Cardinal entered the city and saw the streets covered with dead. He refused to treat Guiton as mayor and ordered him to dismiss his official attendants on pain of death. Richelieu did not show himself cruel in the hour of victory. There was no proposal to suppress Protestant worship, though such a step would have been very popular at court ; provisions were sent into the city quickly and the lives of the remnant were thus saved. It would have been easy to make out a case for the punishment of Guiton ; but he was left unharmed. The story is told that he was asked whether he wished to become a subject of the King of England. He replied, " I had rather serve the King who was able to take La Rochelle than him who could not save it." He died in the naval service of France.

When Richelieu ordered the armed men of La Rochelle to leave the city there marched out sixty-four Frenchmen and ninety Englishmen. That was the force that had latterly been blockaded by an army of 25,000 ! Of the rest at least 10,000 had perished out of a population of 25,000.

The Duke of Rohan was still at large in the south-east of France. Richelieu followed the policy of Henry IV towards the Leaguers and encouraged individual surrenders. Many prominent persons came in and received the pardon of the King. Rohan appealed to King Charles I saying that they had taken up arms " on his advice and promise." But how should England which had failed on the sea-board help in the valleys of the Rhône and Garonne ? Then, when English help had clearly failed, Rohan took a strange and fatal step. He turned to Spain, to the great Catholic power, to the power that had supported the League against Henry of Navarre, to the power that was most closely associated with the Inquisition, above all to the power that was the chief enemy of France and Richelieu. A treaty was made whereby Spain was to give the Huguenots a large subsidy of money, and they promised " to support all the designs of his Majesty the King of Spain at all times with all their power." It was a step which justified the policy of Richelieu, for it made of the Huguenots a definitely anti-national party. And before Spanish help could come the fighting was over. Privas was taken. Alais was besieged. At first Richelieu refused to treat with the party as a whole and insisted on the surrender of individual towns and nobles. But he was in haste to have done with the civil war and to be free for the great European crisis. He allowed therefore a General Assembly of the Huguenots to be held at Anduze, not far from Alais, and there he dictated his terms (June 1629), which are known as the Peace of Alais. Richelieu represents the Peace as a great triumph for Monarchy and Catholicism. " These gentlemen," he writes, " had put forward great claims ; they wished to maintain themselves in small republics. . . . But now they were forced to accept peace, not on their own terms, but just as it pleased the King to give it them, and not as a treaty but as an act of grace." And it was equally a triumph for the Church. " The Ark overthrew the idol of Dagon. God re-entered in triumph all the places from which His public worship had been impiously banished." An end was made of guarantee towns and places of security ; the Huguenots were forced themselves to destroy all the fortifications in which they had trusted.

But there was another side to the matter. The Edict of Nantes was re-affirmed. The Huguenots still were to enjoy liberty of worship and civil equality. If the terms could have been maintained there would have been no reason to regret the loss of their aristocratic protectors and the special standing which made of them a force outside of the framework of the state. But we know that the Edict had little more than fifty years of life before it ; and it was broken in fact long before it was withdrawn officially.

CHAPTER V

WITH the Peace of Alais the Huguenots disappear
as a political party from the history of France. The
Duke of Rohan withdrew from France and fought
in the Thirty Years' War. He died in 1638 of
wounds received in fighting. Soubise died in England and was buried in Westminster Abbey. Since
the fall of La Rochelle there was no attraction in
the Huguenot body for any nobleman who was
anxious to play an ambitious game in opposition
to the Crown. There were still a good many nobles
who remained loyal to the Protestant cause and
many of them had not shared in the rising of 1627–
29. The family of Ruvigny remained faithful
to the end. One member of it was the constant
deputy and advocate of the Huguenots at Court ;
another held high diplomatic position. Turenne,
the great soldier and admired hero of all France,
was a Huguenot and remained so for many years
yet. The Count of Schomberg—not of the same
family as the Schomberg who held command under
Richelieu at the siege of La Rochelle—held the
highest military commands in spite of his German

birth and his Protestant faith. It would be easy to mention a dozen others of less note. But generally speaking the Huguenot churches could no longer count on the loyal support of their aristocratic members. The real strength of the French Protestants was to be found in the middle and artisan class and its adherents were still well over a million.

The ordinary histories of France therefore take little note of the Huguenots until their attention is suddenly called again to them by the Revocation of the Edict of Nantes and the attack that preceded it. They had always protested their loyalty to France and its monarchy, and the next half-century abundantly showed the sincerity of their protests.

If they had been on the watch for opportunities favourable to revolt they would easily have found them. Three years after the armed movement of the Huguenots had been crushed in the south of France, there was a rebellion against Louis XIII, and still more against his Minister, Cardinal Richelieu, headed by the King's brother, the Duke of Orleans, and Henry, Duke of Montmorency. It does not concern us except that the insurgents tried to make profit out of the religious passions and sufferings of Languedoc and appealed for the support of the Huguenots. But their appeal fell on absolutely deaf ears. Nay, the Huguenots rendered extremely useful service to the royal cause. It was due to the Protestants at Nîmes that the city was preserved to the King. Both Montauban and Privas—formerly so ardent in the defence of the Huguenot cause—now took the side of the King.

The action of the Huguenots was all the more welcome to Richelieu because the rebellious Dukes had found considerable support among the Catholic clergy of the district. He expressed his gratitude to them emphatically.

Then on Richelieu's death there came the upheaval that goes by the name of the Fronde. There was a child King and the Queen Regent's chief minister, Cardinal Mazarin, was unpopular and was believed to be weak. Many elements in French society, which had been held in subjection by the strong hand of Richelieu, joined in an attempt to shake the fabric of the absolute monarchy and to restore the power of the nobles and the Parlements. If the Huguenots had been tempted to join the ranks of the Frondeurs, there would have been nothing to wonder at and little to blame. But in fact they remained quiescent and loyal. The leader of the rebels was the Duke of Condé—the great Condé—whose family had been so intimately associated with the early history of French Protestantism. He laid stress on these memories, and he told the Huguenots that the Queen Regent had promised to revoke the Edict of Nantes. But again there was not the slightest movement in sympathy with these appeals. La Rochelle, Montauban, and other Huguenot towns and districts took a prominent part in recruiting armies for the King and in resisting his enemies. Mazarin was loud and generous in his appreciation of the help which the Huguenots had given him. He called them his faithful flock. He spoke of the pastors of

Montauban as his very good friends. The King's representative said to the Huguenots of Montauban, " When the King's crown seemed falling from his head it is you who kept it there." And no history of the Huguenots can fail to repeat the declaration of King Louis XIV made in May 1652, when at last the Fronde was clearly defeated. " Inasmuch as our subjects of the So-called Reformed Religion (this is the official title of the Huguenots) have given us proof of their affection and fidelity, especially in recent circumstances, which have given us great satisfaction, we wish them to understand that for this reason they will be maintained and kept, as in fact we maintain and keep them, in the full enjoyment of the Edict of Nantes." The declaration was greeted with great applause and gratitude by the Huguenots. To our ears it sounds rather strange that a King should think it worth while to affirm that he intended to observe a law of the land, and especially one which was described as " perpetual and irrevocable."

The thirty years from 1630 to 1660 are reckoned the halcyon period of French Protestantism. The hopes and fears, the sufferings and dangerous ambitions of the civil wars were for ever over. The Huguenots were henceforward a religious body living their life without much regard for the politics and wars of the great world. But it must be remembered that their connexion with the state continued to be a close one. Their ministers received part of their stipends from the state ; representatives of the state had a right to be present at their services ; a deputy represented their cause at Court ; the King's commissioner opened their general synods. They were by no means " a free church " as we should understand the word nowadays. The government had therefore an excuse and a means for constant interference and we shall see that they often interfered. Still during these thirty years the Huguenots were able to live their lives in much peace and security. They were, as we have seen, now mainly a middle-class body devoted to commerce and industry and they flourished exceedingly. It is not difficult to understand the origins of the great wealth which is universally attributed to them. They had been trained in a hard school for three generations ; many of the expensive pleasures of ordinary French society were closed to them either by their own principles or by the hostility of the Catholics. They did not observe the Catholic holidays ; they worked harder and played less than the rest, and the result was wealth which had been honestly gained and was generously used. " The great names of industry and finance—the Van Robais of Abbeville, the Massieu of Caen, the Alison of Nîmes, the Herwarth, the Fromont, the Samuel Bernard of Paris are Protestant names." The hostility which they provoked, and which resembles in so many ways the opposition to the Jews in central Europe to-day, was in part due to the superior financial position which their talents and character had won for them. One of the family of Herwarth became finance minister under Mazarin, and the government offices that dealt with financial affairs were largely staffed by Huguenots. They had their own colleges and schools. The chief colleges were at Nîmes, Montauban, and Saumur, and they were largely attended. At an early date there was some difficulty about the definition of Calvinist doctrine. The rigid antagonism between Calvinism and Lutheranism was no longer maintained, and Lutherans were admitted to communion in Huguenot temples. At the college of Nîmes there was a tendency to look for points of agreement with other bodies who had broken away from communion with Rome, and it was one of the charges brought against them by their Catholic opponents that they were ready to enter into alliance with all the heretics of Europe. The teachers at the Academy of Saumur were said to be tainted with the Arminianism which was gaining so strong a hold on the Calvinist churches of the Netherlands. It was a great period of theological controversy all over Europe and nowhere more so than in France. The Catholic Church in France was full of vigour and the presence of the Huguenot body in its midst was a stimulus to thought and controversy. The Jansenist movement was spreading. It gave great trouble to the official heads of the French Church and was ultimately denounced as heretical, but it is a sign of the great religious activity within the Roman Church. The humanism, represented in a previous period by Rabelais and Montaigne, had few representatives. In the theological controversies the Huguenot ministers could quite hold

their own both in the pulpit and in the Press. The
long rows of their works which may still be found
in theological libraries are rarely disturbed now.
We may note certain names. Chamier was one
of the teachers at Montauban and made himself
well known for his attacks on the Jesuits. There
came from his pen a Latin work in four large
volumes which may be translated " *The Catholic
Array, or the Universal order of battle.*" Amyraut
was at Saumur Academy and was accused of teaching doctrines that varied from the sound faith of
Geneva. The controversy assumed considerable
importance but was in the end suppressed by the
Synod at Charenton, which imposed silence with
regard to questions " which were of no value for
the work of salvation." Dumoulin of Sedan was
another eager champion of Geneva against the
Jesuits. He published a *Defence of the Reformed
Churches of France*, in which he attacked the Jesuits.
These were academic teachers, but the ordinary
pastors contributed their share to the controversies
of the time. Drelincourt was always ready to
attack or defend when the Calvinist faith was concerned. Jean Daillé will come before us again as
the moderator of the last general synod. He wrote
on the Fathers of the Church, but his best known
work was a *Defence of the Reformed Churches*. Two
greater names than any of these, or at any rate two
names that are of more use to the historian of the
Huguenots, are Élie Benoit and Jean Claude : the
first, the historian of the Edict of Nantes whose
five great and sumptuously printed volumes are

the great quarry from which most of our knowledge of the Huguenots during the seventeenth century is derived ; the second, the last minister of the Temple of Charenton, the bold defender of his flock and his faith in their darkest hour, who crossed swords with the great Bossuet when everything was on the side of his antagonist—reputation, official position, and the support of the Crown—and came from the contest certainly unbeaten. We may note in conclusion that the contributions of this generation of Huguenots to art and letters was very small. Palissy and Jean Goujon and Marot have no successors. A latin poem in honour of Gustavus Adolphus is the only incursion into the domain of secular literature that I can find.

We have said that these years were the halcyon days of French Protestantism ; but we must not exaggerate the calm. There was always tension and there was often conflict between the Huguenots and their opponents ; and in conflicts the Catholics, backed by the favour of the state and the force of public opinion, nearly always gained something. There are no great events, but we will select from the pages of Benoit certain characteristic incidents.

After the fall of La Rochelle the Huguenots suffered no serious blow while Richelieu lived. It would be interesting to know what were the real feelings of the great cardinal on the subject of religious toleration. He can hardly have contemplated the permanent existence of more than one religious community in the state. But in his first public appearance, when he spoke for the clerical estate in the meeting of the States-General in 1614, he used words which his later career does not belie. " As for the others who blinded by error live peaceably under the authority of the King, we only think of them to express a desire for their conversion ; which we would promote by our example, by our instruction, and by our prayers, for these are the only arms with which we wish to strive against them." When in 1629 the Edict of Grace was issued, under Louis XIII's name, but of course from Richelieu's pen, it " exhorted the King's faithful subjects of the so-called Reformed Religion to cast aside all passion so as to be more ready to receive the light of heaven and to return to the fold of the Church." He hoped then clearly for the conversion of the Huguenots and, when circumstances allowed, he made some effort to bring it about.

We know little of this project of the Cardinal Minister's except from the pages of Benoit, who wrote after the revocation of the Edict of Nantes, when bitter and undeserved suffering had made him ready to interpret every action of the government of France in the worst possible sense. Richelieu seems to have seriously entertained the scheme, for he employed on it his great agent, Father Joseph, who was always his second self. The general plan was to win over a number of the ministers to the idea of discussion, concession, and reunion ; then to hold a conference in the presence of the King ; and if everything went well to follow the conference by decreeing the reunion of the churches. We know how difficult such projects of reunion are even in our own day, and the religious passions of men were so much fiercer in the seventeenth century that success was probably out of the question. A large number of the Ministers frankly regarded the Pope as anti-Christ, and, while that was so, no " accommodation " was possible. Yet some things made success seem possible. It is interesting that a name almost as great as Richelieu's was interested in the affair. Grotius the great Dutchman and Calvinist laboured for peace in international matters, and the idea of an agreement between the churches naturally appealed to him. He wrote a poem in Dutch, which was translated into Latin, on the Truth of Christianity, in which he urged tolerance and insisted on the common ground between Calvinists and Catholics. Richelieu's effort was therefore entirely in harmony with his wishes. A good number of ministers were also won over in so far that they were ready to take part in a conference and did not repudiate the possibility of concord. Benoit writes with contempt of these men " who allowed themselves to be bewitched by the fine name of concord." But they were by no means all worthy of disdain. There was Petit, Professor of Theology at Nîmes, who all his life sought peace and ensued it and was especially concerned to establish an agreement among the reformed churches. It is said that ninety Ministers were won over to the same side. This was La Milletière. He drew up a plan of agreement in which we are told the vital differences between the two confessions were glozed over and the advantage was given to Rome in every point. Perhaps the scheme deserves a more sympathetic treatment than it has received, but it failed and was certain to fail. The Provincial synods which were to have asked for a conference refused to do so. The project was dropped, but was in Richelieu's mind right down to his death. La Milletière wrote much later—in 1637—a book called *The Road to a Christian Peace*, but it got him into difficulties on both sides. The Sorbonne denounced it ; the Huguenots wrote against it and in the end excommunicated him. He was driven to join the Roman Church, " in order to have a religion of some sort," but remained to the end of his life active in the cause of reunion. It is quite possible that he was something different from the poor creature half-knave and half-fool described by Benoit.

There was too a continual effort made to convert the Huguenots by means of missioners, or *convertisseurs*, as they were called. Their activities have been described with bitter mockery by the Huguenot writers. They were, we are told, nearly always " men of a violent, seditious and hair-splitting character, who tried to excite tumults and provoke attacks in order that they might find occasion to bring charges against the principal members of the reformed churches." And again we are told of their favourite trick which was to ask whether the Huguenots believed that Charlemagne, Saint Louis, and Louis XIII were damned. If the answer was No, the question followed, Why abandon a religion where salvation was possible. An affirmative answer brought the imputation of high treason. It was thought best to answer that the Kings had been saved by a special illumination in the hour of death which had revealed to them the nature of the errors of Rome. A missioner called Véron was especially notorious for his procedure. He would go to the sermons of the Huguenots, as he was by law allowed to do, and would then erect a platform at the temple entrance and attempt to refute what had been said. He was a man, we are told, " sans foi, sans pudeur, sans jugement, sans lettres." Sometimes the Catholics were incited to break into the temples and to destroy the furniture and books. There is obviously strong partisanship in all these stories. The desire to convert the Huguenots sprang from the same motives as their desire to convert the Catholics, and much in those motives was laudable. But no one welcomes an attempt to convert him from his errors. And moreover the missioners were paid by the number of their converts, and aimed as much at bringing the law to bear on the Huguenots as at convincing them of the error of their ways. We can well believe that the results achieved were small. After the beginning of the century the two confessions were nearly stable.

And always the Huguenots knew themselves to be observed by an enemy anxious to seize every opportunity that the law permitted to inflict on them loss and humiliation. Even during this period of quiet we can see the working of the system which led up to the Revocation of the Edict half a century later. The King had sworn to maintain the Edict of Nantes, but the meaning of the Edict was sometimes obscure and its implications were difficult to determine. The leaders of Catholic France with the lawyers at their back were determined to interpret the Edict as unfavourably as possible to their opponents, and to find means of reducing the privileges that they enjoyed. The law courts by no means held the scales of justice even. They often openly aimed at supporting the policy of the government, and, unless the Huguenots were protected by the system of divided chambers, they got short shrift at the hands of their opponents. A few instances must be given to make this plain.

There was the question of the *annexes*. The right of the Protestant ministers to hold services in certain towns was admitted. But could the same minister also go out and minister to small congregations outside of the town in places where Huguenot worship was permitted. The practice was forbidden on appeal, and many churches were closed by the process.

Note next the *Grands Jours* at Poitiers. This was a special tribunal, well known to French history, which controlled a wider area than the individual Parlements, and for the time superseded them. Often these Grands Jours had been used for the terror of offenders too powerful to be touched by the ordinary courts, and they would be so used again. But at Poitiers in 1634 they were occupied almost entirely with the position of the Huguenots. A series of decisions there limited their rights or practices. They might not bury in Catholic cemeteries. They might not ring a bell to summon the faithful to prayer. They might not open schools except by Letters Patent. They might not preach in any houses or buildings which belonged to ecclesiastics. They might not speak of themselves as a church ; they must call their faith " the so-called reformed religion." But the affair that gave rise to most heartburning was the demolition of the temple at Saint-Maixent, a small town on the Sèvre. The procedure was highly characteristic of the methods employed for the next fifty years. It was not disputed that Protestant worship was allowed at Saint-Maixent by the Edict ; but it was maintained that the permission to worship did not carry with it the permission to build a church, and the temple at Saint-Maixent had certainly been built since the passing of the Edict. The great lawyer, Omer Talon, appeared as an advocate against the Huguenots and he used words that deserve quotation. " The Edict exists for the purpose of maintaining the King's subjects in a good understanding, of allowing liberty of conscience, of preventing the introduction of the Inquisition, and of winking at and bearing with something whose existence we regret." Some temples were destroyed on these grounds, and others because they were too near to Catholic churches.

In 1636 an inquiry was held into the character

of the Huguenot liturgy. They were accused of
having dropped a prayer for the King in favour of
one that the King might be induced to listen to
their requests. Their preachers were accused of
having called the church of Rome the idolatrous
Babylon and the scarlet woman, and of having
spoken of the Pope as anti-Christ and the Captain
of cutpurses.

But there is so much more of this sort of thing
to come and in a far more cruel and destructive
form that we may well pass from it now. The
Huguenots were allowed to hold general synods
from time to time, and it is in the records of these
that we get the best and most authentic account
of their life. Several were held during the thirty
years that we are considering and all are full of
interest for our purposes. But it will be best to
look only at the last, which proved also to be the
last ever held under the Monarchy. It was held
at Loudun and represented 630 churches and 726
pastors. The royal commissioner who opened the
synod was an aged Councillor of the Parlement of
Paris, of Huguenot origin and belief, called de
Magdelaine. His address was in great part a
homily on the duty of obedience to the King, and
he took throughout a high dictatorial tone. " It is
the King's wish that no ministers of foreign origin
should be appointed and that no Huguenot children
should study at foreign universities. His Majesty's
will is that none of the deputies should speak of
the infraction of the edict. The Catholics have
more reason to complain of infractions than the

Protestants. Many preachers have not received any licence. Children who go to Catholic schools are excommunicated and so are converts to Catholicism. Charitable funds have been diverted to the support of ministers. Letters from abroad have been communicated to the synod." Such were some of the chief complaints in his speech. The tone is hostile and suspicious throughout. At the end he declared that His Majesty had resolved that there should be no more general synods except by his permission.

Monsieur Daillé the Moderator, or chairman of the synod, replied in an admirable speech insisting on the belief of all Huguenots in the duty of obedience to the King, but urging that the Huguenots stood for what seemed to them more important than life itself, and defending with much boldness the strong language which they occasionally used about their opponents.

Loyal messages were then sent to the King and to his minister, Cardinal Mazarin, and answers were received. Mazarin said, " I ask you to believe that I have a great regard for you, as you deserve by being such excellent subjects of the King."

It will be worth our while to turn over the pages of the Minutes and to see what are the questions that are brought up before the synod. The commissioner had definitely forbidden them to debate questions of policy, and many a debate must have been choked by that prohibition. But some of the commonplace business is of interest to us who want to know what manner of men the Huguenots were on the eve of " the great betrayal." There was a good deal about discipline in morals and manners. From Berri there came a request that Ministers be urged " to keep within the bounds of simplicity and to banish from their sermons the vanity and affectation of modern writers." The Ministers were urged " to enjoin modesty in dress and themselves to set the example." The synod regretted to hear that the Pastors did offend in this manner and that their children sometimes showed an affectation to conform to the world in the fashions that had recently been invented. The students of theology in some academies are said " to allow their hair to grow long, to wear long hanging sleeves, and gloves with fringes and ribbands." They also carry swords and frequent taverns and low company. All which the Synod is sorry to hear. There were also more important questions of discipline. Some provincial synods sent up a request that the article on original sin should be modified, and they were granted some concession. The practice of having a catechism of the whole congregation was proving unworkable, and many asked to substitute an address on matters of faith. The synod also had to consider the question of the observance of Sunday and it took up a strongly Sabbatarian attitude. They are " touched with a keen pain," to hear of what is going on, and they urge an abstinence from work and pleasure in a tone that would have satisfied the contemporary Puritans of England. An attack on the moderator himself, Daillé, was received ; he was declared not to be perfectly sound on the doctrine of grace. But the synod found that the charge was merely vexatious and passed on. At La Rochelle the church asked to be allowed to get rid of their minister. At Sauvetat there was a sharp contest between the gentry and the common people ; we have hints of the same thing in other places. The synod decreed a general fast to be held on March 20, 1660, and arrange to hold their next meeting at La Rochelle. But the meeting never took place. The King vetoed it. The Huguenot Parliament was perhaps too large and representative to please his autocratic mind ; or else it was part of the general policy of cutting down the privileges of the Protestants wherever possible.

The position of the Huguenots must have been exasperating in the highest degree. They had wealth, position, organization, but the world round them regarded them with suspicion and hostility. And worse was soon to come.

CHAPTER VI

THE REVOCATION OF THE EDICT OF NANTES

I HAVE now to tell in one short chapter the story of one of the greatest blunders and crimes in European history. The story is a plain one. Neither the facts, nor the motives of the actors, nor the consequences of the act are seriously disputed. The chief difficulty is to think ourselves back into the minds of the men who carried out the deed.

We miss the significance of the Revocation if we think of the government and the society that were responsible for it as being particularly cruel or unenlightened. The contrary is the fact. The French monarchy under Louis XIV was the most brilliantly successful government in Europe. Its triumphs made men think that only under a concentrated and centralized form of government could a state be really successful, and the English parliamentary system had as yet few admirers. The Court and the courtiers of France raised the standard of manners throughout Europe, and the etiquette of the palace was copied everywhere. The armies of France had won a decided supremacy over all others ; and it may be noted that the two most famous French soldiers—Turenne and Condé

—were both sprung from families of Huguenot origin, and Turenne remained Huguenot until the year 1668.

Nor was the supremacy of France less marked in other directions. It was one of the greatest ages—perhaps the greatest age—of French literature. We need not enumerate the great poets, dramatists, philosophers and historians who made all Europe turn its eyes towards France with envy and admiration. The literature of the time, like all great literature, was widely human in its sympathies, though it lacked the humanism which Rabelais and Montaigne exhibited in the previous century and which Voltaire and Rousseau would show in the next. But if we are inclined to think of the age as harsh and unsympathetic the Letters of Madame Sevigné are enough to sweeten the whole period.

Great in arms and in arts the age was equally distinguished for what it accomplished in the sphere of religion. It marks the zenith of the Gallican view of Catholicism, and in 1682 an assembly of the French Church protested against the Pope's assumption of temporal power and declared that even in spiritual matters his authority was less than that of General Councils. And the French Church was not only famous for its political action. It made great contributions to religious thought and to the literature of piety. Bossuet has attracted the love and admiration of Protestant students. Fénélon's writings have touched the hearts of innumerable readers both inside and outside of his

143

own communion. Pascal's relation to the official Church was uncertain, for he belonged to the Jansenist body whose movement was bitterly opposed by the Church and state in alliance. But he ranks as one of the greatest of modern religious philosophers. It was too a great age of preaching, and the sermons of Bossuet, Bourdaloue and others were as popular as theatrical representations. Unquestionably the Catholic Church contributed in this era more than the Protestants of France to the permanent religious thought of Europe.

The whole of this magnificent state revolved round the King and received its impulse from him. No one in all history has lived in an atmosphere of more shameless flattery, and no doubt it had its effect in numbing his moral sensibilities and in blunting his judgment. There are in his private life and in his public life actions that are bound to provoke condemnation—quite apart from the Revocation which we shall soon consider. As to his character and abilities, men will never agree ; but to me it seems that he had many fine qualities, a real sense of duty to his people and to France, and even a touch of heroism in the time of disaster. His political and diplomatic ability, especially in the latter part of his reign, was certainly great.

It was a state brilliantly successful in every direction that inflicted on the Huguenots this cruel torment and on itself a deadly wound. For what reasons ?

The Huguenots were no longer dangerous. Mazarin had called them his docile flock, and their docility had never altered during the fifty years that preceded the Revocation. The governments of the sixteenth century were to some extent excused, by the real dangers that menaced them, for the measures that they took against the Huguenots. Louis XIV's government can claim no such excuse.

The Huguenots contributed much more than their proportional share to the wealth and commercial development of France, which was so great a concern of the King and of his first great minister, Colbert. Their overthrow was a blow to the commercial prosperity of France from which it did not recover before the Revolution.

They had ceased to proselytize. Any attempt to do so would have been severely punished. Their numbers remained stationary with doubtless some tendency to diminish. They did not challenge the official Church in any way, and they vied with it in preaching the duty of obedience to Kings and governments under all circumstances.

Why then did France inflict such torture and humiliation on a religious body which hurt neither Church nor state in any way, and helped them, if they could but have seen it, in many ways ? It is somewhat difficult to find the answer.

Many causes contributed to the tragedy. The passions of the last century survived into very different circumstances ; for now men were beginning in various parts of Europe to explore the possibilities of religious equality, and France herself had had experience of its benefits. But heresy was still to churchmen not merely an evil but the greatest

of evils. When Louis XIV had cast aside the
excesses of his early reign and turned to religion
with a genuine devotion the extirpation of heresy
seemed to him the best way by which he could show
his repentance and his zeal in the service of God.
The Church never failed to demand with horrible
iteration the curtailing of the liberties of the Huguenots which seemed to them an insult to their
Church and to God. There was no one with the
sanity and political instinct of Richelieu to point
out the dangers of such a procedure and to recom-
mend the way of peace. It was above all to a false
idea of unity that the rights of the Huguenots and
the prosperity of France were sacrificed. Political
and religious ideas here worked hand in hand. As
I read the edicts which were issued against the
Protestants of France I am again and again reminded of the treatment of the Jews in Germany of
to-day.

In 1652 the King had issued a welcome declaration that he would observe the Edict of Nantes.
But even before the death of Mazarin the process
of interpreting the Edict, always in a sense unfavourable to the Huguenots, had begun, and from
the first Louis XIV wished it to go on. There is
a passage in his *Mémoires* written for his grandson
which has often been quoted, but which must find
a place here : " I thought that the best way to
reduce little by little the Huguenots of my kingdom
was at first not to use against them any new severity,
and to maintain all the concessions which they had
obtained from my predecessors, but to give them

nothing more and to limit the execution even of these within the narrowest bounds that justice and decency (*bienséance*) would admit. But as for the favours that depended on myself alone I determined, and I have exactly maintained this decision, to grant them none. And that I did out of kindness, not out of harshness, in order to force them to consider, of their own accord and without any violence, whether they had any good reason to deprive themselves voluntarily of the advantages which they might have enjoyed in common with all my subjects." Clearly the King thought of Protestantism as a foolish fancy, the product of egotism and obstinacy. He and the leaders of the Church believed that it would give way without much difficulty to a certain amount of pressure. He probably never knew the real nature of the compulsion that was used.

The years from 1660 to 1679 were the most prosperous of the whole of his very long reign. Colbert was making changes and reforms in the administration of the finances which were long overdue, and he made much use of the Huguenots as his agents and clerks. The foreign policy of France followed at first the lines that had become traditional since the sixteenth century. Spain was the enemy in the first war, which added a coveted slice of the Belgian lands to France. In 1672 Louis took a step which marked a great change in the diplomacy of Europe and was the prelude to the disasters of the last years of his reign ; for in that year he declared war against the United Netherlands. It had been by French help rendered by diplomacy, by money, and by arms that the Dutch had been able to gain and to keep their independence. When France drew her sword to destroy them the whole diplomatic chess-board of Europe was disarranged. But Louis did not thereby entirely abandon the system of alliances with Protestant powers which had been the mainstay of French power for a century ; for France was allied with England and was anxious for the support of Denmark, Prussia, and Sweden. The foreign relations of France remained therefore so far favourable to the Huguenots that they made any declared attack on their position under the Edict of Nantes unlikely and politically inexpedient.

None the less these years saw a worsening of the position of the Huguenots. They found themselves in face of a large hostile majority, which was backed by all the forces of the state, and supported by the King himself. There was no obscurity or conceal-ment about the intentions of their adversaries. It never entered their imaginations that the Edict of Nantes was an honour and a strength to France ; they never dreamed of accepting any measure of religious equality as a permanent part of the life of the state. The Huguenots were heretics, and, as they would not accept the King's religion, they were nearly rebels as well. They broke the unity of the state ; they were a scandal and a danger. Religion, policy, and morality all demanded the weakening of their power and if possible their destruction.

And if the intentions of their enemies were plain so also were the means that they proposed to employ : and even during this comparatively happy period the means were employed with effect.

First came the interpretation of the Edict. It was by no means a well-drafted document. It was the work of opportunism in the higher sense of the word, and shows clear traces of the difficulties experienced in passing it on to the statute book. There were alterations and additions made at the last moment. Many of the clauses are really difficult to understand. There is no declaration of principles such as is found in the much finer Peace of Monsieur in 1576. The Edict stood in real need of interpretation—but of something quite different from what it actually received. Many took a hand in the evil work. There was Filleau, a lawyer at Poitiers and a declared opponent of the privileges of the Huguenots. He published in 1661 a book called *Catholic Decisions : A General Collection of the Verdicts given in all the Sovereign Courts of France in execution or Interpretation of the Edicts which concern the So-called Reformed Religion.* Then there was the Jesuit Meynier who wrote in 1663 a book, *Concerning the Edict of Nantes,* in which he pointed out the ways in which the Edict might be so interpreted as to yield very little protection to the Huguenots. He was followed by Bernard a lawyer and judge in the Presidial court of Béziers, who wrote in 1664, *Maxims to be observed by the Executive Commissioners of the Edict of Nantes in their Decisions* ; and in 1666, *An Explanation of the Edict of Nantes by other Edicts of Pacification and Regulative Decisions.* This last was the great manual of the persecution. And these men were only giving definite form to the wishes of the General Assembly of the clergy of France. For the persecution was not the work of the King and government or of some one order or group of persons. It was quite definitely the work of the Church in France as a whole. The clergy of France held their General Assemblies from time to time, and they dealt with various matters ; but I think they never failed in any one of their meetings to demand some blow against the Huguenots. What the clergy demanded to-day the King performed sooner or later. They covered him with flattery after the manner of the time, but they called on him as a thanksgiving to God " to employ his authority for the extirpation of heresy " and thus to emulate the fame of " Valentinian, Theodosius and Charles."

We must see something of these methods of interpretation. It was assumed in the first place that the Edict—though called in the preamble perpetual and irrevocable—" had been extracted by force of arms from the indulgence of Kings who were constrained by the necessity of the times," and was a temporary measure to maintain peace, while means for the restoration of religious unity were being prepared. And on this basis it was safe to assume that the King intended to give as little as the words of the different clauses could be made to mean. M. Bernard's Maxims do not reach quite the full growth of his final book, but they will show us clearly the kind of procedure that he advocated. Thus Article IX of the Edict reads : " We permit those of the afore-mentioned religion to hold and continue its exercise in all places of our obedience, where it was by them established and publicly held on several different occasions in the year 1596 and in the year 1597 up to the end of the month of August." The wording is somewhat confused, but its meaning is plain. The problem before Filleul, Meynier, and Bernard was to find in it a means not of maintaining but of destroying the Huguenot churches of France. The word " established " gave them the necessary lever. What is the essence of establishment ? Not mere existence by any means. No ; in order to be established a church must be publicly opened : it must send members to the provincial synod : it must have a consistory. And then the word " publicly " ; what is the precise meaning to be attached to that ? It is not enough that baptisms should have been celebrated and that sermons should have been preached, if these things were not done publicly. It is not enough that religious service should have been held regularly. It must have been public ; known, that is, to all the neighbourhood, to the Catholics as well as to the Huguenots. We need not pursue the argument further. Many churches were destroyed on grounds such as these. Article X of the Edict was even more open to attacks of this kind. " Religious worship may be established also in all towns and places where

it was established or ought to have been established
by the Edict of pacification of the year 1577."
Nearly a hundred years ago ! How difficult and
indeed impossible to determine exactly the conditions of so remote a period ! We need go no
further into the Maxims. We cannot accuse Élie
Benoît of exaggeration when he says that all might
have been reduced to a single maxim. " There
can be no title so clear or definite as to avail in
favour of a hated party whose ruin has been sworn ;
and the lowest and grossest tricks are welcome if
they afford grounds for condemning heretics."
The Maxims or the policy behind them were by
no means without effect. Even before 1579 we
have constant mention in the records of churches
destroyed on these or similar pretences. The
inquiry into the affairs of the Huguenots was given
to two commissioners ; the one the King's all-
powerful intendant who represented the majesty
of the King in the provinces ; the other some
Huguenot chosen by the Crown, who if he had
been the worthiest representative of his faith could
hardly have made his opinions avail against his
official colleague. And too often the Huguenot
representative was chosen for his servility, and
sometimes he had actually sold himself to the
government.

There is another document which will show us
the spirit in which the government regarded its
relations with the Huguenots. On February 1,
1669, there came a Declaration of the King " laying
down the things which must be kept and observed

by those who make profession of the R.P.R."
There are forty-nine regulations. A few—a very
few—take the side of the Huguenots in unimportant
matters. From the large number I will extract
those which show the petty interference and ignominious treatment which the Huguenots received,
by order of the King, at the hands of his officials.

Where noblemen hold Protestant worship in their
houses there must be no public sign of the worship.
(3) Ministers visiting prisoners may only give them
religious consolation in a low voice and in such a
way as to avoid scandal. (4) Ministers may not
use in their sermons terms insulting or offensive to
the Catholic Religion or the state. (5) Ministers
may not call themselves Pastors of the Church but
only Ministers of the R.P.R. (7) Ministers may
not wear gowns or cassocks or appear in long robes
elsewhere than in the temples. (8) Ministers may
not preach in different places, but they must live
and preach only in the place assigned to them by
their synods. (13) No colloquy may be held except
while a synod is being held, and no synod may be
held except by royal permission. (16) Ministers
and others may not sing psalms when illuminations
are made in public places by royal orders, nor when
criminals of their confession are being executed.
(19) The following are the regulations for the
funerals of Huguenots in the country. From the
month of April to the month of September the
funeral processions shall start precisely at six in
the morning and at six at night ; and from October
to March at eight in the morning and four at night.

They shall proceed continuously with the numbers allowed by royal decrees. (22) In Languedoc and Guienne, where there are two consuls and one is bound by law to be a Huguenot, the first consul must always be a Catholic even though the Huguenots are in a majority in the place. (27) When the Holy Sacrament being carried in procession passes before the temples of the Huguenots they must cease to sing their psalms. (31) Children whose fathers are Catholics and whose mothers are Protestants shall be baptized in the Catholic Church. (39) Huguenots may not expose meat for sale on the days on which the Church orders a fast. (47) Bells in Huguenot temples may not be rung between Maundy Thursday and Easter Eve. It is fair to add that there are four clauses which contain some regulation favourable to the Huguenots, but they do not alter the general character of the regulations.

The Catholic Church in France was constantly invoking the interference of the law and the government against their Protestant opponents, but they recognized the need of other methods more suited to religious controversy. Louis XIV, in the extract from his *Mémoires* which we have given above, thought that the Huguenots would be brought over to the Church when it became clear to them that their material interest pointed to such a course. But the Church did not neglect argument and exhortation and it was at the moment particularly well supplied with champions to represent it in debate. Especially Bossuet was at the zenith of his powers. He was a really great scholar. His eloquence was passionately admired, though it is too elaborate and self-conscious for modern taste. His life was free from reproach, and he had a remarkable gift of clear and convincing exposition with a perfect control over his temper. What champion could the Huguenots bring forward against this splendid advocate ? Their ministers must have appeared like dogs fighting with lions ; but they did not decline the contest. Victory was in the circumstances impossible, but they acquitted themselves with honour and courage and often seem to the modern reader to have the best of the argument.

Until 1668 the fact that Marshal Turenne was a member of their communion was of the greatest importance to the Huguenots. For even in his lifetime he was almost a mythical hero to the majority of the French people, and even now it would be hard to find anyone who approaches so nearly to the model " that every man in arms would wish to be." His family had given much to the Huguenot cause and, though his connexion with it must have been always largely traditional, he had resisted all attempts to induce him to leave the religious body in which he had been brought up. Then in 1668 came the news that he had yielded and had been received into the Catholic Church. The causes of his resolution were and still are variously interpreted, but a large part was usually ascribed to Bossuet. If Turenne had given way, who could stand firm ? He had a niece, Madame Duras, who hesitated many years as to whether she should follow her uncle or not. In order to assist

her in making up her mind a colloquy was arranged
in her presence between Bossuet and a representative of the Huguenots. They had as their champion Claude, the Minister of the church at
Charenton, the nearest church to Paris, where no
Huguenot building was allowed.

Bossuet had devoted much thought and energy
to the controversy with the Huguenots. It was for
them—and especially for Marshal Turenne—that
he had written his *Explanation of Catholic Doctrine
in Matters of Controversy*, which shows his style
and his powers of argument at their best. His aim
was to reduce the points at issue between Catholics
and Huguenots to the narrowest limits and to
present them in a tone so conciliatory and charitable
as to make further consideration of them easy ;
and the book had a considerable effect. It was
natural therefore that Bossuet should be chosen for
this rather theatrical debate with Claude before
Madame Duras and certain other courtiers.
Bossuet published his own account of the debate
and Claude charged him with having broken his
word in doing so. There had been, he says, an
understanding that nothing should be published.
He felt constrained, however, to publish his own
account to correct that of Bossuet.

The duel was an interesting one. It took place
in February 1678 ; on the eve, that is, of the determined offensive of the government against the
Huguenots. It will therefore be of interest to note
the general character of the principles advanced on
either side. The debate was entirely devoted to

theological and ecclesiastical questions. Of the great social, political and even international issues that were involved there was no hint. Both debaters accepted the literal authenticity of the Bible, and a good deal of the contest is singularly meaningless to modern readers. Bossuet's contention is simple. There must be and there always has been an infallible authority in matters of faith ; before the coming of Christ the authority was the synagogue ; since the inauguration of the Christian era it has been the Catholic Church ; those who reject that authority are inevitably plunged into religious anarchy. He summed up his thesis in conversation with Madame Duras, and the following sentences are taken from that summary. " God wished his children to have an easy means of deciding all that belonged to their salvation. This means is the authority of the church, a means easy to establish, easy to understand, easy to follow. . . . To this church belongs the communion of the saints, the remission of sins, the resurrection of the body and everlasting life. Outside of this church there is no communion of saints, no remission of sins or resurrection to eternal life. . . . The Scriptures without their proper interpretation are a dagger to murder us (*un couteau pour nous égorger*). God forbid that the church should give us the Scriptures without explaining them to us."

Claude has given us his account of the debate and has also published at great length his comments on Bossuet's main theses. He recognizes the great qualities of his adversary : " I observed in him an

extraordinary candour and civility of behaviour."
His account of the debate corresponds closely with
that given by Bossuet. He confronted the arguments of his adversary with great strength of conviction and lucidity of reasoning. At one point
he seems to the modern reader to come near gaining a dialectical victory, when he asks how Christianity could have come into being if the authority
of the synagogue had been accepted as final. His
central contentions are : first, that Protestantism
is no new thing but a continuation of the Christian
Church of earlier times purged of its errors ;
secondly, that by the church is meant not " an
external and visible company " but something more
mystic and spiritual. It is only fair to give two
short quotations. First as to the continuity of the
Christian Church. " Is there any necessity that a
church should groan under the same oppression in
order to be the same with a church that was before ?
The Protestants have not one jot the less really
and truly a succession of sees, of councils, and of
the profession of religion for not having that part
of them which was earthly and unclean. The
vessels of the temple are the same, only they are
washed, made clean, and restored to their natural
use." And next as to the meaning of " the church."
Bossuet had defined the church as " A Society
making profession to believe the doctrine of Jesus
Christ and to govern itself by His word." Claude
would substitute : " A Society of such persons as,
making profession to believe the doctrine of Jesus
Christ, do truly and effectually believe it ; and

making profession to govern themselves by His word do really and effectually govern themselves by it. We are concerned to know," he adds, " whether the nature and essence of the church consists barely in externals and appearances or whether something of reality be not also required." He found more difficulty in dealing with Bossuet's attack on the consequences of private judgment.

If the controversy was to be settled by intellectual and moral arguments we should be ready to admire the calm, luminous methods of the great Bishop as well as the honesty and determination of his adversary. But, while Bossuet quoted texts and appealed to the teaching of church-history, other weapons were preparing. The Huguenots were not to be persuaded by argument or weaned from their faith by the example of a good life. They would be harried by unjust laws, hounded like untouchables from the commercial occupations in which they were so distinguished, outraged in their homes by a brutal soldiery, driven into the living death of galley slaves, massacred by thousands in the mountains of the Cevennes. And, though Bossuet's noble nature would have shrunk with horror from many of the enormities that were practised, he must bear part of the responsibility for urging the government to extirpate heresy if need were by violence.

1579 is usually taken as marking a turn for the worse in the treatment of the Huguenots. For one thing France then entered on a period of peace. The Peace of Nimeguen had brought the Dutch war to an end. It had been a hard-fought struggle, for the Dutch had in the end found allies to support their own determined resistance. France had by no means gained all that she had hoped, but her soldiers were unbeaten and her territories increased, as the result of more than six years of fighting. The King and his government had leisure at last for domestic problems. And the extirpation of heresy had long been foremost on the programme. It was the fate of the Huguenots that events which have many admirable features turned to their undoing. There was a change in the character and life of the King, very much for the better, if we considered only his private life. The early part of his reign had shown even more licence than history is accustomed to in the lives of Kings. Mistresses one after the other had held an almost official position at Court and, though the life of the palace had always a certain decorum and splendour, serious interests, except so far as they concerned war and finance, found little place in his attention. But there had always been a strong religious strain in the King's character and interests, and this now began to come into prominence. It was not a sudden conversion. Even after the change was well marked in him he had occasional returns to his old ways ; but the tendency strength-ened until it was completely triumphant. It is closely associated with the name of Madame de Maintenon. This most interesting woman was the grand-daughter of Agrippa d'Aubigné, the Huguenot, who played a prominent part in the reign of Henry IV, and she had herself been brought up in the Huguenot faith. She had emigrated with her father to Martinique, and he had died there. She was then placed in Catholic surroundings and was brought up as a Catholic. She had married when she was only seventeen the dramatist Scarron who was a cripple and forty-two. As the head of his household she received many people of note in letters and society, who admired her beauty and her behaviour in her difficult position. She was left a widow in 1660 but still held a place in the world of fashion and the Court. She knew the King's mistress, Madame de Montespan, and it was in her rooms that she met the King. In 1669 he asked her to become governess to the children that Madame de Montespan had borne him, and after some hesitation she consented. It was the beginning of one of the most amazing careers that have fallen to a woman. The King, as was natural, saw her frequently and found her conversation a welcome contrast to what he was accustomed to, for they talked of religion. We cannot follow one of the best-known stories in history. Under her influence, the King dismissed his mistress and was reconciled to his much-injured wife, who expressed her warm gratitude for Madame de Maintenon's services. Then in 1683, when the Queen, Marie Thérèse, died, Madame Scarron became the wife of King Louis XIV ; the ex-Huguenot and widow of a playwright became the wife of the most magnificent King in Europe and perhaps in all history. She was his wife, but not the Queen

of France. The marriage was celebrated with all
the forms required by the Church, but Louis XIV
never acknowledged her in the eyes of Europe, and
perhaps it was impossible according to the ideas of
the time that he should do so. We must not think
that the King was dominated by Madame de Maintenon—he was too strong a character to be dominated by anyone. But she powerfully assisted a
change which would perhaps have come in any
case. The Court became religious and moral.
Attendance at Mass, instead of at private theatricals,
became the best road to the King's favour. There
is much that is attractive in the life that the King
lived with his wife, though the courtiers ridiculed
behind his back his obvious devotion to a woman
very different from those that had previously
reigned in the salons of the palace. But in the
seventeenth century and in France to love religion
was to hate heresy, and to hate heresy was to seek
to destroy it by any means. In 1679 Madame de
Maintenon had written—in words on which the future
was to make a terrible comment—" The King is
full of good feeling. He sometimes reads the Bible
and finds it the most beautiful of books. He admits
his weakness and recognizes his failings. We must
wait for Grace to work upon him. He is thinking
seriously of the conversion of the heretics, and will
soon set to work at it earnestly." The same tone
and thought appears in a letter written by her in
1681. " The King is beginning to think seriously
of his salvation, and, if God preserves him to us,
there will soon be only one religion in the kingdom."

During this time the King and the Church in France had a sharp contest with the Pope on the question of Gallican liberties. Some foolish people even said that France would go the way of England and set up an independent national Church, though of that there was never really any chance. But the debate was keen, and in 1682 there came the famous declaration of Gallican Liberties, which said among other things that the authority of Councils was superior to that of the Pope. But even this quarrel was rather a danger to the Huguenots than a help. Louis and his Bishops wished to show that their claims for the customs and practices of the Church in France were not tinctured with heresy, and their difference with the Pope made them the more anxious to belabour the Huguenots.

From 1679 the attacks on the Huguenots became constant. Between that year and the withdrawal of the Edict of Nantes in 1685 there were more than a hundred and twenty-five documents of different kinds dealing with the Huguenots, and all of them curtailed their liberties or inflicted on them penalties of some kind. They were not blows struck in blind hatred of heresy, but reveal a carefully thought-out system and almost a science of persecution. There were no dramatic martyrdoms ; no victims invoking the name of Christ from the midst of the flames. Heresy was not made a legal offence ; it might be claimed that no person was punished because he was a Huguenot. Privileges were withdrawn ; means of livelihood were taken away ; the stigma of social inferiority was attached in every way ; the Huguenots became almost untouchables. When finally the Edict was withdrawn it was nominally the wiping from the statute book of provisions that were no longer needed because the Huguenots had practically ceased to exist. It is easy to recite the long list of edicts and regulations which did the evil work, but it is only by an effort of the imagination that we can realize what it all meant for the victims. A community above the average of their fellow-citizens in education, in industry, in thrift, and self-reliance were treated like hunted animals, round whom their pursuers gather in ever closer and closer circles until at last they rush in and give the final blow.

No summary of these hundred and twenty-five laws and regulations can give the effect that they produce when read *in extenso* and in order : but they can only be summarized.

1. The Huguenots were excluded from all public employments. The Edict had given them civil equality and equal admissibility to all posts. But the King could appoint whom he would, and a series of edicts shut them out from all judicial appointments both high and low ; from all posts in the financial administration where they had done such excellent service ; from all posts on the estates of the high nobility ; from posts in the royal household.

2. The professions of medicine and law were largely in their hands and their exclusion from official posts would make them the more eager to

enter these professions. But one royal declaration forbade them being admitted into the legal profession—justifying the veto by the fact that they had already been excluded from the higher judicial posts ; and another, confessing naïvely that the profession was so full of Huguenots that there was a danger of Catholics being excluded altogether, ordered that for the future no Huguenot should practise medicine. They were also forbidden to print or to sell books.

3. The legal guarantees were taken from them, as the military had been by Richelieu. The courts of the Edict, on which there were bound to be Protestant as well as Catholic judges, were suppressed one by one, on the ground that religious animosity was dead and they were therefore no longer needed. After this there was hardly a pretence of even-handed justice when Huguenots were litigants. The Archbishop of Arles declared that this would make more conversions than all the preachers and missions in a century.

4. The Huguenot family was attacked from many sides. Mixed marriages were forbidden. No Huguenot might be a midwife. But the worst was a declaration of the King dated June 17, 1681, written in a tone of the most abject hypocrisy. It regrets that children have not been allowed to participate in the " great success which it has pleased God to give to the spiritual incitements and other reasonable means which we have used for the conversion of our subjects," and declares that children may *at the age of seven* declare them-

selves converted to Catholicism and claim from their parents a reasonable pension. Conversion was proved on the slightest and most absurd evidence, and the opening that this law gave to fraud and cruelty can easily be imagined.

5. Direct financial pressure was ruthlessly employed. Converts to Catholicism were relieved for three years from the payment of their debts and for two years from the payment of the *taille* and the obligation to give lodgings to soldiers. As early as 1676 an ex-Huguenot called Pellisson had established a fund for the purchase of conversions, which he himself administered with much pride in his invention. We can easily imagine the mean chicanery which surrounded this expedient.

6. And all the time the destruction of temples and the suppression of Protestant worship went on apace. New reasons were found for destroying the temples. Catholics went to the sermons to watch for a slip. If the preacher used any word that could be twisted into a reflection on the King or the King's religion, if he even spoke of " the misery of the times," that was enough ; the temple was destroyed. Any temple which admitted within its walls a convert from Catholicism was destroyed, though the identification of such converts was often impossible. Many temples were pulled down because there were too many of them for the needs of the district. If a temple was destroyed the Huguenots were not allowed to worship on the site under heavy penalties.

There is no end to the regulations and laws

which enclosed the Huguenots on every side. But there was one method of enforcing conversion of horrible efficiency, which must not be forgotten. We know in English history of the seventeenth century how loud were the protests called out by the billeting of soldiers on private persons, and that the evil was not abolished until the Revolution of 1688. Events in France supply a commentary on this phrase, and perhaps partly explain the bitterness of the opposition in England. In 1680 the intendant Marillac went into Poitou accompanied by priests and dragoons—soldiers, that is, who could fight on horseback or on foot. He billeted them exclusively on the Huguenot population, and in a year he obtained 30,000 conversions ! The figures are perhaps more expressive than any details. Élie Benoît fills several pages with instances and stories of the cruelties that were committed. The financial burden was crushing and conversion at once relieved the victims from the obligation of supporting the soldiers and also from the need of paying certain taxes. But the real pressure was not financial ; it lay in the brutalities of the soldiers which were encouraged by the authorities. Property was destroyed and stolen ; old men, women and children were cruelly ill-used. The habits of soldiers in Europe in the seventeenth century were never of the best—the influence of the Thirty Years' War was still felt in that matter—and discipline was difficult to maintain. But the dragoons were encouraged to ill-treat those on whom they were billeted. The story was current that when the troops entered a village the priests encouraged them to do as much harm as they could. " Courage," they cried, " for it is the wish of the King that these dogs of Huguenots should be well plundered and punished." The story may not be literally true, but it represents accurately enough the spirit of the proceedings.

" As patient as a Huguenot " had passed into a proverb, but there were some who could not endure the injustices inflicted on them without an effort at resistance. It was in the lower valley of the Rhône that these troubles were at their worst, in the Vivarais and in Dauphiné, in the Cevennes and in Languedoc. They were the result of despair, for there was not the slightest chance of renewing the civil-religious wars on a large scale. There was a little fighting followed by much punishment. " La canaille," as Louvois called the Huguenots, was severely punished, many temples were destroyed, and an excuse was given for further severities.

The year 1685 opened with the worst auspices for the Huguenots. The Crown of England was soon to pass from a concealed to an open adherent of the Church of Rome. There was no help for the Huguenots to be expected from any foreign power, and in France their fate had been determined.

At the beginning of 1685 the Huguenots addressed to the King an appeal drawn up by Bossuet's old adversary, Claude, with dignity and moderation. They recalled the solemn promise given them by Henry IV and repeated by Louis XIII in the Edict of which : " only the trunk remains, the leaves and branches having been all cut away." They admitted with sorrow the share that they had taken in the rebellions against the Crown " seduced by the influence of the nobles or constrained by the necessity of defending their own lives " ; but they recalled with pride their defence of the monarchy against the Catholic League and their loyalty during the Fronde. They hear it constantly said that " in the interest of the state there ought to be only one religion, and that it will redound to the glory of his Majesty, being as he is all powerful in his kingdom, to reduce all to the one Catholic religion." But they maintain that religious toleration becomes just and necessary, when it is guaranteed by law, and when it cannot be withdrawn without inflicting suffering on a great many of the subjects of the King. Moreover, " religion has its seat in the soul and cannot penetrate there except by way of persuasion and prayer. Methods of force only make atheists and hypocrites and rouse in those of good faith a courage and perseverance which makes them despise punishments." The King acknowledged the receipt, but made no further reply. He continued to repeat right down to the end that he intended to observe the Edict of Nantes.

With or without his knowledge the final attack on the Huguenots was being arranged. Laws and penalties, bribes and rewards had done much : but the soldiers had done most in the past and they were to be used for the *coup de grâce*. Marillac had been withdrawn and even censured for his work in Poitou, but now his methods were continued and developed. Poitou was visited again, but the great arena of battle was Béarn, once one of the great strongholds of French Protestantism. There was tension with Spain and a considerable force had been sent into Béarn in order to be ready to strike if an armed demonstration were decided on. The danger of a Spanish war passed, and the troops were employed against the Huguenots. Foucault the intendant directed the operations. They are known as the dragonnades, because something in the name or the dress of the dragoons specially caught the fancy of the public, but every part of the army was equally concerned in the work. Béarn had already been cruelly handled and its temples had been reduced to five, and those were in places difficult of access. A Bishop made a public declaration that it was the King's wish that all his subjects should be Catholics. Then the troops were let loose upon those who refused. Élie Benoît devotes two chapters to the enormities committed in Béarn and other provinces. It would be painful and useless to give details ; we may hope that there are many exaggerations. But there is no ground for distrusting the following general statement. " The Intendant led them from town to town and from village to village. They entered everywhere sword in hand ; they were billeted only on the Protestants ; they lived as they liked and were guilty of every inhumanity which brutality, fury and rage can commit when supported by authority. They carried out these cruelties not only by the permission but by the express order of the Intendant, who taught them new means of breaking down the most stubborn patience." Conversions were reported by tens of thousands. The King was delighted with the result. He called it a success " very useful for our religion and a very good example for the other provinces of my kingdom."

Other provinces were not slow to copy the example of Béarn. The troops marched into Languedoc and into Guienne. There was no escape, and there is no reason to wonder that vast numbers pronounced the words or signed the papers which were necessary to save them from brutal ill-treatment and even from murder ; the wonder rather is that so many remained firm. A new feature in this period was the surrender of whole towns to the religious demands of the troops. Thus the Duke of Noailles wrote to Louvois, the powerful minister of war who took a chief part in directing the attacks on the Huguenots : " The most prominent people in Nîmes abjured their religion in the church the day after my arrival. There was subsequently a little falling off, but things went well again after I had lodged some troops with the most stubborn. The number of sectaries in this province is about 240,000 and I think I shall have done with them before the end of the month."

The Edict was, however, still " maintained " : though it had ceased to protect life or liberty or property. Should the farce continue ? The situation would be simpler and in some ways easier if it were abandoned. The ministers of the cult could not well be banished while the cult remained in existence and the ministers were believed—probably rightly—to be the great supporters of Huguenot resistance. (Louvois says that the desire to banish the ministers was the real cause of the formal revocation.) The pecuniary privileges too of the new converts were so extensive as to be a real burden to the state. It would be easier to treat all Frenchmen alike if there were no legal Huguenot body left in France. So the Chancellor, Le Tellier, the father of Louvois, drew up the edict for the Revocation and submitted it to the King. He made a few changes and sent it to the Parlement of Paris for registration. They had refused for long to register the Edict of Nantes, but they welcomed its destruction. From October 22, 1685, there was only one religion in France !

The Act of Revocation deserves the same attention that we gave to the Edict of Nantes itself. The introduction is a strange document and has been called by the great historian Lavisse " a shameful page in the historical documents of France." Henry IV, it says, had granted the Edict to give peace to France and to allow mutual animosities to die down " in order that he might be in a better position to labour for the reunion of those to the church who had so lightly separated from it." His death had prevented him from doing anything, and Louis XIII had been too constantly engaged in wars. Louis XIV too had found no time sufficiently free from troubles until the year

1684. All he had been able to do " for the advantage of religion " had been to diminish the
number of temples and to abolish the divided
chambers " which had only been set up provision-
ally." " But now we see with thankfulness to God
that our cares have had the end we proposed for
them, since the better and the larger part of our
subjects of the R.P.R. have embraced Catholicism."
Wherefore the Edict of Nantes is hereby revoked
entirely. There follow certain detailed clauses.

(1) All temples are to be destroyed at once.
(2) No Huguenot service is to be allowed on any
pretext in any public place or private house. (4)
Ministers who will not accept conversion must
leave the kingdom within ten days on pain of the
galleys if they are found in France after that date.
(5) Ministers who will accept conversion are to
have a pension one-third larger than their former
stipend and (6) are to be admitted to the legal
profession on easy terms. (8) Children born to
Huguenot parents are to be baptized by Catholic
priests and brought up as Catholics. (9) Huguenots who have fled from the country are invited to
return. But if they don't their property is to be
confiscated. (10) Huguenots are absolutely forbidden to leave the country or to send out their
property on pain of the galleys. A last general
clause assured those who still remained faithful to
the R.P.R. that they would be allowed to live
freely in all lands within the limits of the royal
obedience, without being troubled on account of
their religion, on condition that they did not hold

any service or meet for any religious purpose. " Car tel est notre plaisir." Signed Louis and sealed with the great seal of green wax.

There is no more painful and melancholy story than that which reaches its culmination, though not its end, in the Revocation. There are stories of religious persecution more cruel and murderous in the records of Spain, of Germany, and even of England ; and certain features of the treatment of the Huguenots were reproduced and perhaps copied in the Irish penal statutes of the eighteenth century. But the cruel treatment of the Huguenots is specially deplorable, because France had led the way towards a better attitude towards religious dissidents by the Edict of Nantes. She had had experience of the working of freedom and a measure of equality, and might have convinced herself of its advantages. Moreover, she was soon once more to be leading Europe towards humanity in law and religion, for Voltaire was born in 1694. The eminence of the great churchmen of France make the crime all the greater ; it is almost incredible that the thing was done with the approval of the Church that counted Bossuet, Fénélon and Saint Cyran among its members. The religious unity that was the chief motive for the infliction of all this suffering was by no means attained or only for a short time. The sufferings of the Huguenots gave a weapon into the hands of the " philosophers " of which they were not slow to avail themselves, and soon France led the way toward that very religious anarchy that Bossuet so much feared.

For the moment there was nothing heard but loud eulogy of the Revocation. This was inevitable. Enthusiasm for the monarchy was so great and the habit of flattery so deeply ingrained that courtiers and writers vied with one another in praising the decision of Louis XIV to get rid of heresy from the soil of France. We need only quote the words of Bossuet in his Funeral Oration on Le Tellier, the Chancellor who had drawn up the Act of Revocation and who died immediately after its publication. The dark shadow cast by the Revocation was not yet apparent, and Bossuet gave full course to his fervent enthusiasm. " Let us make known the miracle of our times ; let us make known what we feel about the piety of Louis ; let us raise our acclamations to the skies ; and let us say to this new Theodosius, this new Marcian, this new Charlemagne—Here is the glorious accomplishment of your reign ; it is this that gives it its true character ; by your deed heresy exists no longer ; God alone has wrought this miracle."

But events soon made this tone rather difficult. For in the first place heresy had not disappeared from the soil of France. The words of the Act which had promised freedom of conscience had been welcomed by great numbers as meaning that the persecution was over, if only they abstained from public worship. Many of the new converts thought it safe now to withdraw the abjuration that they had made under compulsion and to return to their old co-religionaries. They were soon undeceived as to the security which the Act gave.

Louis XIV believed that there were practically no Huguenots left in France and his agents were concerned to justify this belief. The dragonnades had to begin again and the cruelties were even greater after the Act than before. On various pretexts great numbers of Huguenots were punished and sent to the galleys. But it was clear that there remained in France hundreds of thousands of Huguenots who cherished in silence bitter animosity to the government of Louis.

A large number of Huguenots, however, found life in France no longer tolerable. Many had fled before the Revocation, but still more defied the prohibition of the Edict and all its penalties and crossed the frontiers after it had been promulgated. No one puts the number of emigrants lower than 100,000 ; some have thought that nearly half a million left France ; the generally received figure now is in the neighbourhood of 250,000. Vauban, so famous as a military engineer and so interesting for his social and economic speculations, wrote soon after the Revocation that France had lost 100,000 inhabitants, 9,000 sailors, 12,000 veteran soldiers, 600 officers and her most flourishing manufactures. The thought of the blow that the suppression of the Huguenots would inflict on manufactures had prevented Colbert from joining in the work and had even roused scruples in the breast of Louvois. And what France lost her neighbours and rivals gained. The Huguenot refugees poured into Switzerland, into Holland, into Prussia, into England. The beginning of the greatness of Berlin is ascribed to the arrival of these intelligent and industrious colonists. They were welcomed in England with an effusion which may remind us of the enthusiasm shown for the Belgian refugees at the beginning of the Great War. More than twenty churches—no longer temples—were opened for them in London, and the district of Spitalfields was largely peopled by silk-weavers of Huguenot origin. They made their way too to the English colonies in America, though they were of course excluded from the French colony in Canada, and settled in considerable numbers in the Dutch possessions in South Africa. They carried everywhere their energy, their language and culture, and the tradition of hostility to the French monarchy and its policy.

The Revocation, too, coincides with a great change in the foreign policy of France and in her military fortunes. She had since the sixteenth century been usually in alliance with the Protestant powers of Europe. She had contributed to the rise of Holland ; the *entente* with England had been sometimes broken but remained a general feature of her policy ; with Prussia she had been usually on excellent terms. From this time onwards she has to encounter the constant opposition of England, of Prussia, and of Holland until the reign of Louis XIV closes in the disasters of the War of Spanish Succession. All this must not of course be attributed to the influence of Protestantism or to indignation with the treatment of the French Huguenots. The change had already begun and would probably have developed in any case. But the deed so rapturously praised by Bossuet, and doubtless carried out by Louis with the firmest conviction that he was doing something at once righteous and serviceable to his country, was a powerful contributory cause of the disastrous change in the fortunes of the country.

The feeling of France soon began to change. The consequences, financial and political, could hardly be mistaken. There was too—it is a relief to record it—a section of religious opinion in France which was shocked by some features of the new settlement. The gentle Fénelon could hardly fail to be offended by the dragonnades and the driving of the Huguenots into religious ceremonies which they detested. Even Benoît gives instances of kindness shown by the religious orders to some distressed Huguenots. But the official utterances of the Church in France remained hostile to all concessions to the Protestants for yet another century. Right down to the very eve of the Revolution, while the most dangerous attack against Christianity in every form was being made by the philosophers, the leaders of the French Church seemed still to regard the forlorn remnants of the Protestant congregations as their chief enemy and to demand the maintenance of all the cruel measures that had been passed against them.

Among modern historians the act of Louis XIV has found no defenders. French historians are not one whit less vehement than English or Americans in condemning the motives and the consequences of the King's act. The Age of Louis XIV has, of course, many admirers and defenders, and the character of the King is now—I think justly—regarded with more sympathy and approval than was once the practice. But even those who regard the Grand Monarque as " the highest type of the Latin that the world has ever seen," who think him fundamentally " tender-hearted and sympathetic " and " at heart demo-cratic " can find nothing to praise in his religious policy. At most they can lay stress on the fact that France was not alone in harrying religious dissidents and can point to evil deeds done in Holland, England, Ireland, and elsewhere. They may speak of the deed as inevitable, as something that even Henry IV if he had lived would have been bound to carry out (a most doubtful judgment), but none can refuse their admiration to the patience and endurance of the Huguenots or their con-demnation to the policy that turned these admirable men and citizens into exiles and outcasts and made them the enemies of the land that they had not ceased to love.

CHAPTER VII

THE HUGUENOTS OF THE DISPERSION

THE pressure exercised by the French governments on the Huguenots had induced many of them to emigrate even in the sixteenth and early seventeenth centuries. Holland, Germany and England had groups of foreign Protestants long before the Revocation of the Edict of Nantes. The increasing severity of the religious coercion in France during the twenty years that preceded the Revocation had vastly quickened the movement of emigration ; and, when the Revocation came, there was a general inclination among the Huguenots to find, outside of the France which they had loved and served well, a home where they might live and work in peace without renouncing their faith. The King's Edicts forbade the Huguenots to emigrate—except their ministers who were formally banished. But their life in France had become so full of suffering and danger and ignominy that the flight could not be stopped and was hardly checked.

We saw in the last chapter that France had lost at least a quarter of a million of her citizens. They were of varied character and occupations ; but their value to the development of the state was greater than is implied by the mere number. The vastly important work that Colbert had undertaken for the industrial development of the state had depended largely on them. France had challenged, and perhaps had won, the leading place among the manufacturing nations of Europe. The trade in silks and in woollens had been principally in their hands. Administration, commerce and banking depended very largely on men of Huguenot stock. The fact that they were excluded from so many careers made them all the more energetic in those that were left open to them. A surprisingly large number of them were in the army, and Vauban has spoken in high terms of their skill and spirit. A quarter of a million of these men were flung by the policy of Louis XIV among the Protestant nations of Europe, who were soon leagued against him in a war which lasted under different names for a quarter of a century. This long, exhausting and unsuccessful war is itself one of the chief causes of that decline in the prosperity and prestige of France which is so marked a feature of the end of the reign. But the Revocation was an important subsidiary cause of the war and contributed very much to the failure of the arms of France, if only because it caused the serious impoverishment of the country. These general results of the Dispersion have already been glanced at. In this chapter I shall try to show the chief routes taken by the refugees in their flight and the characteristics of their settlement in the various countries.

1. *The Netherlands*

The connexion between France and the Netherlands had been very close for centuries. The success of the rebellion of the northern provinces against Spain in the sixteenth century was in no small degree due to the help which they had received from France. Henry IV and Richelieu had both contributed to the work. Louis XIV himself had at first been friendly. It was natural therefore that the chief current in the Huguenot emigration should take the direction of Holland and the Netherlands. It is estimated that 100,000 Huguenots reached Holland, while England and Germany are reckoned to have received about 80,000 each.

It was perhaps fortunate for the Huguenots that Europe still showed signs of the desolation which the Thirty Years' War had spread. In parts of Germany there were fertile lands which had fallen out of cultivation and towns which were in ruins. Even in the United Provinces there were waste lands, where the help of the exiles was welcomed.

Since the war of 1672 the government of the Netherlands had regarded Louis XIV with great suspicion and hostility. The events of that year had brought William of Orange to the head of the state and his whole career was inspired by a passion of hatred for France and her ruler. It was natural therefore that the Huguenots in their cruel ill-treatment at the hands of the French King should find sympathy and support from the Dutch. The emigration into the Netherlands had begun many years before the Revocation. The stories of the persecution were eagerly read and circulated and the cruelties of the dragonnades perhaps exaggerated. The French ambassador at The Hague complained of an "atrocity campaign" which was being conducted against France, though in his private letters to the King he urged some modification in the treatment of the Huguenots on account of the bad impression that it was producing. The policy to be adopted towards the Huguenot refugees was a matter for the individual states of the federation not for the central government. Several states invited the Huguenots to settle in their midst in the most cordial terms. The city of Amsterdam gave to Huguenot immigrants full rights of citizenship, the right of exercising any trade or profession without further formality, and freedom from city taxes for three years. The government of the state of Holland exempted them from taxes for twelve years. The Estates of Friesland declared in language that sounds strangely to the ears of the twentieth century that, "inasmuch as the welfare of countries doth herein consist that the same be populous," they were determined to grant to all foreign families whom stress of religious persecution had forced to leave their homes every right enjoyed by natives. Both before and after the Revocation great numbers arrived and they soon exercised an important influence on the policy and life of the state. The first result was to embitter the feeling of the Dutch against Louis XIV. William of Orange was confronted by a party which wished to establish more friendly relations with France and shrank from the prospect of another war. The arrival of the refugees was a serious blow to this party. The Great King's policy was apparently directed towards the destruction of Protestantism everywhere, and the country generally adopted a mood of warlike suspicion which much assisted the designs of William, when in 1688 he entered on the great adventure which gave him the Crown of England, and plunged Europe into a war that marked the beginning of the decline of the fortunes of Louis XIV. The refugees, moreover, especially the first swarms, were not destitute men who needed to be supported. They brought with them much wealth and so great was the influx of capital into the Netherlands that the rate of interest sank to little more than half. French money helped William to embark for England. There were Huguenot soldiers with him when he landed in Torbay. Huguenot regiments served with him at the Battle of the Boyne and supported the allies in their struggle against Louis XIV, until the Treaty of Utrecht in 1713 marked the definite overthrow of his schemes and hopes. There can be no question that in military science and *morale* France had been for half a century ahead of the rest of Europe. It was partly through the refugee soldiers that the methods of Turenne and Vauban passed over to the enemies of France.

A new vigour was infused into the commercial and industrial life of the Netherlands by the refugees. There was at first no jealousy felt towards them. They had trade secrets which the Dutch were very glad to share. Trades which had hitherto been a monopoly of the French ceased to be so now. The French ambassador was constant and loud in his reports of the serious blows that were being struck against France by this process. The silk trade, so carefully fostered by Henry of Navarre and so skilfully conducted by French manufacturers, had sent its products throughout Europe and had brought great wealth to France. But now every branch of it was brought to Holland by French workmen and masters. The cloth trade too was stimulated by the new arrivals, and new processes were taught to the Dutch workmen. The manufacture of felt hats had been a flourishing trade in France, but now hats of all kinds were made in Amsterdam, and the Comte d'Avaux recounts with sorrow that they were even being imported into France. It was Amsterdam more than any other city which profited by the new methods. " All these industries have been established in two years and without expense—on which the greatest ministers of the very Christian King (of France) have spent many millions. The city is thereby filled with inhabitants, the public revenues are increased, its walls and its boulevards are enlarged. Money circulates, new buildings are erected, commerce flourishes, the Protestant religion is strengthened, all countries come to trade. Amsterdam has become one of the most famous cities in the world and resembles the ancient city of Tyre, which the prophet called 'perfect in beauty.'" There is clearly some exaggeration in this, but a great change was passing over not only Amsterdam but over other cities of the Low Countries as well. The French were good farmers too and had something to teach the Dutch even there. It is especially noted that they brought with them a taste for gardening and taught the Dutch to cultivate "roses, carnations, and honeysuckle." But here the pupil has outstripped the master.

The religious and intellectual life of Holland soon showed strong traces of the French influx. In 1688 there were sixty-two churches wholly or mainly devoted to the French refugees. The number of ministers who found a home was especially large and they exercised a great influence on the religious life of the country. France was in the seventeenth century the great home of preaching as a fine art, and the Huguenot ministers had caught something of the methods of Bossuet and Bourdaloue. Their passionate eloquence and impressive gestures were something new to the more phlegmatic Dutch and stimulated a new interest in religion and its controversies. Many of the best-known names among French divines enjoyed the hospitality of the Dutch at this period. Saurin was the greatest of the preachers, and the specimens of his pulpit eloquence substantiate the claim that in him Bossuet had a worthy rival. Claude, the minister of Charenton, who had crossed swords with Bossuet himself, came to Holland after the Revocation and died at The Hague in 1687. It was there that he published his *Plaintes des Protestants de France* which had a European circulation and did much to reveal the true character of the means employed to suppress Protestantism in France. Élie Benoît too, whose *History of the Edict of Nantes* is the great quarry from which historians must draw their details of the persecution, settled in Holland, and there published his work in five magnificent volumes ; it is amazing that so splendid a specimen of printing, binding and book production could have been remunerative for such a work. But in the time of the war Benoît's book was a means of propaganda and was bought and circulated for political reasons.

It was not only theology and preaching which were stimulated by the arrival of the Huguenots in Holland. They had not of late made much mark in literature and science in France, but it was apparent that the reason was to be found, not in any lack of talent, but in the refusal of the government to admit them to academic and professional life. Now natural history, medicine and mathematics all received an impulsion from them. Jacques Bernard was a great mathematician. Lyonnet was a naturalist of note. Both were Huguenots. But for the history of thought the greatest name among the French settlers was Pierre Bayle. His relations with Calvinism had been equivocal. He was the son of a Huguenot minister, but at the age of twenty-two he abjured Protestantism and joined the Roman Church, being impressed by the need of authority in matters of religion. He was not, however, happy in his new surroundings, and after a study of the writings of Descartes he rejoined the Protestant communion. He had taught at the Huguenot University of Sedan, and when that institution was suppressed he had moved to Rotterdam in 1681. It was there that he wrote his bitter denunciations of the methods used by Louis XIV in " making France wholly catholic," in which he maintained that it was not Catholicism or Christianity of any kind that would profit in the long run by the action of France. It was Deism, he said, that would triumph not Catholic orthodoxy. " The outside world," he wrote, " thinks that God is too essentially good to be the author of so evil a thing as positive religion." And again addressing the rulers of France he said : " I pity you for your rejection of the spirit of Christianity. But I pity still more Christianity itself, which you have made to stink, if I may use the expression of the Gospel, among the other religions." Bayle's is too important a name to be treated merely in relation to the Huguenot movement. His own speculations were sceptical and carried him far away from the doctrines which Calvin had preached at Geneva. They brought him into sharp conflict with ministers and supporters of the old doctrines. But what he said about the effect of the Revocation on religious thought was true and important. It gave a most powerful stimulus to the tendency of French humanists to break away from all forms of established religion and to find the basis for their hopes in vague Deism.

It is interesting too to note that some hundreds of Huguenots accepted the offer of the Dutch Government to carry them to the Cape of Good Hope and establish them there. They settled by the Berg River to the west of the Drakenstein. They called their home La Perle, but it was later perverted under Dutch influence to Paarl. They applied themselves to farming and organized their religious life in the familiar way. Their numbers were not large enough to allow them to maintain their language, and they soon came to adopt the prevalent Dutch ; but their names and something in their customs and even in their dress for long bore witness to their French origin. In the Great Boer War French names among the Boer forces recalled the influence of this strain, which had contributed a valuable element to the life of the colony.

2. *Great Britain*

No country had watched the treatment of the Huguenots in France with more interest than England. The relation between the English and French Crowns had been intimate ever since the Restoration. The example of Louis XIV's government had a great influence on the policy of Charles II, and though opinion had compelled the King to renounce the French alliance the friendliness between the two royal families had hardly been interrupted. When James II embarked on his plans for the exaltation of the power of the monarchy against that of Parliament, and the removal of the unjust disabilities under which the Roman

Catholics of England suffered, he was bound to be drawn into close co-operation with the French King, however much he resented the patronage and offers of help which came to him from Paris.

The Huguenots had begun to pour over into England as soon as the policy of Louis had taken a decided turn against them in 1680. They were generally welcomed both out of religious sympathy and because it was quickly seen that their arrival would tend to the increase of English trade and manufacture. In 1681 there was a collection made for necessitous French Protestants, and a royal proclamation promised them " all privileges and immunities for the liberty and free exercise of their trades and handicrafts." The declaration was received with passionate gratitude by the refugees and a minister addressing Charles II declared, " We love you as a God on earth, for such you are." James II as an honest and determined Catholic was thrown into a great dilemma by the flood of exiles that followed the Revocation. He was advocating the principle of religious toleration in the interests of the Roman Catholics and couldn't repudiate it when it was claimed by the Huguenots. But on the other hand their presence and the stories widely circulated of the cruel treatment which they received in France made his schemes for the admission of the English Roman Catholics into the body politic more difficult of acceptance. So his actions with regard to the distressed fugitives were equivocal. He allowed a collection to be made for them in all churches ; but he ordered Claude's book on their sufferings to be burnt and he encouraged the French ambassador in his attempts to induce them to return.

The Revolution of 1688, which put on the throne of England a Calvinist and the greatest opponent of Louis XIV in Europe, completely altered the situation. The Huguenots were welcomed now with enthusiasm and came in numbers greater than those which were attracted by any other country except Holland. The immigration never lost its strongly religious character. Churches, consistories and ministers were the inevitable features of their settlement. Soon there were twenty-one churches—for they were no longer called temples—in London alone, as well as many in various parts of England. A constant feature of the time was the repudiation by Huguenots, who under pressure of persecution had renounced their faith, of the Catholicism which they had for a moment pretended to accept. But London was by no means alone in welcoming them. There was hardly a considerable town in England that had not its French colony. Southampton, Canterbury, Bristol, Norwich are specially mentioned for their hospitality to the new-comers. Calvinist Scotland naturally opened its arms to them, and a French colony in Edinburgh is said to have used the French language until the middle of the eighteenth century. The situation and character of Ireland made their treatment there more questionable. Ulster was friendly ; the government at Dublin was ready to welcome them, but the great mass of the population would have no special sympathy for them or their sufferings. Moreover, Ireland was the scene of much fighting and the disturbed condition of the country made it unattractive to peaceful immigrants. On the other hand, the troubles of the seventeenth century had left much of the country desolate, and the English Government saw in the immigration of French Protestants a means of giving Ireland prosperity and strengthening the Protestant element in the population. There were French groups at Dublin, Cork, Waterford and Lisburn, but the most interesting settlement was at Portarlington under the protection and influence of the Marquis of Ruvigny. He had received large grants of land for his services to William III, and he planted there by the banks of the Barrow four hundred French emigrants and built for them a church and a school. The Huguenots soon passed beyond the limits of Great Britain, and emigrated to the American colonies. The French Government had been ill advised in excluding Huguenots from their colonies, for they were an ideal material for colonization. Now the loss of France was the gain of England. They went by choice to the colonies of the south, to Virginia and to Carolina, where the names of Charlestown and of Carolina itself recalled the early efforts at French colonization under the French King, Charles IX. But they were found also in the northern colonies and they prospered everywhere.

They were received with open arms in England and, although there was later some jealousy of them, and their ways were not exactly the ways of the English of the seventeenth century, there was on the whole wonderfully little friction between the new-comers and the natives of the different parts of Great Britain. Their military aid was of great value. We shall see how Cavalier, the leader of the Huguenots in the Cevennes, entered the English armies and rendered excellent service. Ruvigny, the son of the Marquis who had for many years been the representative of the Huguenots at the Court of Versailles, served the Protestant allies for many years with equal distinction as soldier and diplomat. But the most notable soldier transferred by the Revocation from the armies of France to those of her enemies was Schomberg. He was a German and belonged to the ducal house of Cleves. He had joined the French armies in 1650 and had been recognized as a worthy rival and colleague of Turenne and Condé. He had left France at the Revocation and had attached himself to the fortunes of William III. He landed with him in Torbay, fought for him in Ireland, and was killed at the battle of the Boyne. The best-known story of that battle tells how the Huguenots under Schomberg found themselves opposed to the French regiments that fought for James. Schomberg called on his troops to muster all their courage and to remember their grievances. "There are your persecutors," he said, pointing to the troops of the French King.

The great services rendered by the French refugees to manufactures in England is well known. They settled in great numbers in Spitalfields and the adjoining districts of London ; a large quarter of London was for generations markedly French in character. The industrial supremacy of France passed over to England with their arrival ; all the elaborate protective schemes of Colbert were defeated at once by the flight of the best workmen of France with their secrets and their skill. It is possible to make out a long list of the occupations which were introduced or improved by the industrious and skilful French. Watches, knives, locks, surgical instruments, hats, paper—all these were made by the French immigrants who from the first associated Englishmen with them in their work. But it was in the production of certain wearing materials that their activity was most marked. Satin, velvet, brocade, linen were all made by them. The silk trade, which had been almost a French monopoly, was introduced by them and soon became a valuable part of the wealth of England. The gain of England and Holland was exactly reflected in the loss of France. There were manufacturing towns and districts that were left deserted. France lost a revenue of nearly two millions sterling by the failure of her export trade in silks and linen. It is hard to find in history any other instance of so wanton a blow struck by a ruler against the prosperity of his own country.

3. *Brandenburg-Prussia*

The flight of the French refugees to Holland and to Great Britain was for the most part spontaneous ; but there was one great European state which devoted much energy and thought to attracting them within its frontiers and superintending their settlements. This was the great Electorate of Brandenburg, which soon, in 1700, assumed the name of the Kingdom of Prussia. No country had suffered more from the ravages of the Thirty Years' War than this. The great city of Magdeburg had been twice destroyed and was still a heap of ruins far shrunken from its former importance. The fields had been left uncultivated for many years and many were so still. Nowhere were the industry and skill of the French more welcome ; nowhere did they produce more obvious and permanent results.

The ruler of Brandenburg in 1685 was Frederick William, known to history as the Great Elector and often called the founder of modern Prussia. He was connected by many ties with France and especially with the French Protestants. His house had been Calvinist since 1614, though the population of the electorate was for the most part Lutheran. His wife was the granddaughter of William the Silent and the great-granddaughter of Coligny, the noblest of French Huguenot leaders. French soldiers and teachers had already found a welcome in his dominions.

The greatness and prosperity of his state was his master passion ; and he realized that the lands between the Elbe and Oder were in many respects behind the development of western Europe. He was quick to see the chance afforded by the Revocation of the Edict. Exactly a week after its publication the Elector issued the Edict of Potsdam. Its preamble expressed in the clearest terms the sympathy of the Elector for the sufferings of the Huguenots. " As the persecutions and the cruel treatment, practised for some time past in France against those of the Reformed Religion, have obliged many families to leave that kingdom and to seek a home in foreign countries, WE, touched by the just compassion which we are bound to feel for those who unfortunately suffer for the Gospel and for the purity of the faith which we confess in common with them, have determined by the present Edict, signed by our hand, to offer to them a free and safe retreat in all the lands and provinces beneath our sway and to make known to them the rights, liberties, and advantages which we wish them to enjoy here, in order to console them and to compensate them in some degree for the calamities with which it has pleased Providence to inflict so considerable a part of his church."

Then follow the practical proposals. The representative of Brandenburg in the United Provinces will provide them with ships and provisions to allow them to travel to Hamburg, where they will be forwarded to any city or place in the Electorate which they may select. Another depot for dealing with the refugees will be established in Frankfort-on-the-Main where ships and money and passports would be ready for them if they wished to pass farther within the territories of the Elector. They were to be allowed to go wherever they pleased, but certain places were mentioned as being particularly suitable for them and ready to receive them : Stendal, Werbe, Rathenau, Brandenburg, Frankfort, Magdeburg, Halle, Kolbe and Königsberg. " WE have given order that as soon as any Frenchmen shall arrive there he shall be well received and arrangements shall be made for all that is necessary for his establishment, but he shall have complete liberty to decide for himself what city or province within our estates is most suitable for them." Their property was to be free from all taxation : ruined or empty houses were put at their disposal ; wood, stone, bricks, lime and other materials were to be provided them and for six years they were to be free from all taxes and from the billeting of soldiers. They were to be received at once into all trades, guilds and trade corporations without the payment of entrance fees, and were to be treated from the first as the natural subjects of the Elector. Industrial workmen and agricultural labourers were to be specially welcomed. If any controversy arose between a Frenchman and a German it was to be settled by the local magistrate, acting conjointly with someone chosen by the French themselves from their own number. A minister was to be established in each town and a church assigned to him. The French nobles were especially welcomed into the army. Not only the stipulations of the Edict but the language in which it is expressed makes it a wonder of generous hospitality. Nor was it merely a sudden act of enthusiasm. It was carefully thought out and followed up by carefully detailed arrangements. The Elector knew that his sadly impoverished state would not be able to meet the needs of the new-comers by taxation or would resent it if they were asked to do so. He provided for them to a large extent out of his private purse and established a bank to make loans to the most necessitous. He believed that their industry would soon repay the money that was spent upon them.

The work done by the refugees in Brandenburg was not different in kind from what they did elsewhere, but it was more definitely organized by the state and can therefore be traced more easily. French soldiers were eagerly received and were given rank equal or superior to that which they had enjoyed in France. It is especially noted that they brought with them the system of fortification, which Vauban had elaborated in France and which had been so important a cause of the victories of the early part of Louis XIV's reign. Schomberg, whose services to England we have already seen, went first to Brandenburg and, though he stayed there but a short time, signalized his stay by the creation of a body of " grands mousquetaires " after the pattern of the French mousquetaires. They consisted entirely of gentlemen and officers. Trade was stimulated by the new-comers, as it was in Holland and in England. Industries unknown before appeared between the Elbe and the Oder. Articles of convenience and luxury were introduced to the simple population of Brandenburg. The devastation of the Thirty Years' War was to some large extent retrieved by the French immigrants.

The effects on two cities are especially noticeable. Magdeburg had suffered perhaps more than any other considerable city in Germany. Under French influence its houses were restored, its streets again occupied by a busy population ; it could soon be called " one of the strongest and most flourishing colonies in the state," and was especially remarkable for the woollen industry which the French introduced. Still more remarkable was the effect on Berlin. In 1685 that city was far from being one of the greatest and most famous of European capitals. The beginning of its greatness is traceable to the influence of the French. All the trades which were practised by the French—we have given a partial list of them in speaking of England—were soon to be found in Berlin, and they were directed and controlled by the Elector with the minute care which had been used for the planting of industries in France by the great French minister Colbert. It has often been noted that there was something " Prussian " about Colbert, and his example was readily followed in Prussia. M. Weiss, the historian of the dispersion, sums up the effect on Berlin in the following words : " The total number of Frenchmen who established themselves in Berlin during the last fifteen years of the seventeenth century reached not less than 10,000. They contributed to the transformation of this city, which previously resembled a dirty stable inhabited by a few thousand cattle breeders, into an elegant capital adorned with sumptuous palaces and convenient houses with a population that rose rapidly from

7,000 to 27,000 inhabitants." When we reflect on all that Prussia has meant to France, and Berlin to Paris, it is strange to note how much was contributed to the growth of Prussia and Berlin at a very critical moment by these refugees from France.

French culture and French scholarship came as well as French military and industrial science. Foreign doctors were eagerly welcomed. The French language became fashionable at Court and spread widely among the middle class. The movement was thus begun which assumed such importance in the days of Frederick the Great. The Germans have themselves not been slow to recognize the great services which the clear and cultivated intelligence of France rendered to the development of the thought and culture of Germany.

4. *The Emigration Elsewhere*

Holland, England, and Brandenburg were not alone in receiving the fugitives from France. All Protestant countries welcomed a certain number on their territory. Some of these emigrations have many interesting features, but all must be summarily treated here.

The Swiss lands (the republic of Geneva and the Swiss Confederation) had counted for much in the history of Protestantism, and especially of French Protestantism. In the western districts there were large numbers of French-speaking people. It was therefore inevitable that when the persecution became hot in France large numbers of Huguenots found their way across the frontier to safety in

Switzerland. The districts of the Pays de Gex and Bresse had been annexed to France by the diplomacy of Henry IV. Their population was almost wholly Protestant and their religion had been guaranteed to them at the time of the annexation. But they suffered the same oppressions as the other Protestants of France, and they knew that the dragoons were coming to convert them. They abandoned their country and in some instances burned their houses and crossed the frontier into Geneva in great numbers. Eight thousand arrived in the course of five weeks. On November 24 a service was held in the great church for the refugees and filled the building. Many merely passed through Geneva into eastern Switzerland or Germany, but many remained. Their presence provoked the angry attention of Louis XIV. " You will declare to the magistrates of the city," he wrote to his representative there, " that I will not allow them to continue to give protection to any of my subjects who desire to leave my kingdom without my permission." He threatened to break off commercial relations with Geneva, if his wishes were not complied with. The little republic was too weak to resist openly. It is one of the miracles of history that a state so small, so important, and so bitterly hated, should have survived and should never have been absorbed in one of the neighbouring monarchies. But, though the refugees were officially ordered to leave, the city connived at their continued residence. When the European war came in 1688 Geneva was protected by the allied powers. The French immigrants continued to form a recognizable section of the population for two centuries.

Bern was the strongest and proudest of the confederate Swiss states, and she had been identified with Protestantism almost from the beginning of the movement. Many thousands of Huguenots made their way there. In the story of their relations with the natives we meet a circumstance which occurred indeed elsewhere, but is on the whole strangely absent from the history of the settlements in other countries. The arrival of these thousands of poverty-stricken refugees in need of subsistence and clamouring for work raised difficult economic problems, and their presence was by no means welcome to the workmen of a state that had not suffered so severely as many from the devastations of the Thirty Years' War. A great number of them were passed on into Germany and Brandenburg-Prussia.

The Scandinavian states of Denmark and Sweden were less ready to offer an asylum to the persecuted Huguenots. Religion and policy both contributed to this result. For both states had adopted the Lutheran form of Protestantism, and it had become decidedly hostile to all that derived from Calvinism. A Danish bishop protested against the policy of " a mixture of religions," and another preacher contrasted Lutheranism, which easily accepted the principle of absolute monarchy, with Calvinism founded on opposite principles. Denmark too was an ally of France and received a pension from the

French King. But in consequence partly of the pleading of the Queen of Denmark the refugees were admitted and formed settlements at Copenhagen, at Altona, and at Fredricia. Louis tried to induce Huguenot officers to leave the service of England or Holland and to take service with Denmark by promising that such officers should be allowed to enjoy half of the income from their properties in France. It is interesting to note that some Huguenots passed into Iceland and introduced there the manufacture of flax and hemp.

Some hundreds of refugees made their way to Sweden or to the German lands under the dominion of Sweden. Still farther afield Peter the Great saw in these French exiles the very material that he required for his great plan of introducing western ideas into his territories. We hear of 4,000 French soldiers in a Russian regiment. There was a French Protestant congregation at Saint Petersburg to which Geneva sent a minister.

There has perhaps been a tendency to exaggerate the effect of the French exodus. It is true that France was not the only civilized country in Europe in the seventeenth century ; it is true too that even if the Huguenots had not been driven out France would have been faced at the end of the seventeenth century by dangers that she could have hardly surmounted. But the spread of French culture, French industrial processes, and French refinement by the Huguenot exiles is a fact of great importance for the history of civilization in the next century. And when in 1713 France by the Treaty of Utrecht had to admit defeat and saw herself exhausted to the point of collapse and deprived of valuable territories, the cruel and senseless treatment of the Huguenots by Louis XIV was one of the important contributing causes.

CHAPTER VIII

IT was the assumption of Louis XIV and of his advisers that with the withdrawal of the Edict of Nantes French Protestantism had come to an end. The majority and the better section of them had accepted Catholicism ; those who still remained stubborn were ignorant eccentrics, who would soon yield to persuasion or at any rate would die out with the lapse of a few years. Many saw with genuine and deep enthusiasm and gratitude the restoration of religious unity in the land and they welcomed it both on political and religious grounds. The few " temples " still left standing were destroyed with many signs of rejoicing. France was free henceforward from the stain of heresy.

The facts were something very different from this official rose-coloured version of them. There remained still in France hundreds of thousands who had not consented to abjure their Protestant faith ; the majority of those who had abjured resented the compulsion that had been used against them and retained an affection for the communion which they had left and in many cases an ardent longing to return to it. The government of Louis XIV—

the strongest government in Europe—proved un-
equal to the task of treading out the embers of the
despised faith. They continued to burn. Soon a
bright flame was visible in several parts of France.
It continued to burn and to spread until in about a
century the government of France had to recognize
and to tolerate the existence of a religious movement, which had been declared to be extinct. The
new Protestant Church was in some ways different
from the old ; especially it had fewer adherents in
the upper classes of society ; but it remained an
important element in the life of the French people.

This is the really heroic chapter in the history
of the Huguenots. The great movements of the
sixteenth century were tarnished by aristocratic
ambitions and political aims. In the seventeenth
century the Huguenots seemed sometimes to accept
the action of the government rather too tamely in
the hope of retaining what remained to them of
their liberties. But in the eighteenth century they
had nothing to hope for from the government.
The movement became as purely religious a movement as is to be found in history. They received
no effective help from the Protestant powers of
Europe. It was their own courage and their refusal
to be untrue to the truth as they saw it which
carried them through many sufferings to security
in the end. It used sometimes to be maintained
that there was not in the French character the stuff
of which religious martyrs are made ; and that the
Puritan outlook on life with its strength and weakness is essentially alien to the French temperament.

But that view must be abandoned. Puritanism was born in Geneva and its parents were French-men. The enthusiasms, the sufferings, and the courage of the Scotch Presbyterians and Cameron-ians can all be paralleled from the records of French Protestantism in the eighteenth century. A modern French historian [1] writes, " The Calvinist minority by reason of the purity of its morals, the active intensity of its religious life, and its energy of character was truly an élite, whose soul had perhaps been made hard and sombre but had also been finely tempered by the persecutions of a century." It was the Puritan element which the French King was expelling from France and from all influence on French life. English history will suggest to us how much was lost when the spiritual kin of Milton and Cromwell and Bunyan were treated as outcasts.

The tragic-heroic story of the Huguenots during the eighteenth century must be told in the slightest outline.

When the first raptures and mutual congratu-lations were over, the government of Louis XIV found itself faced with a difficult and at the same time an absurd situation. By the tenth clause of the Edict of Revocation Huguenots were expressly forbidden to leave the country (except their minis-ters, who were banished). But as we have seen in the last chapter they escaped from France by the hundred thousand. The fugitives themselves could not be brought back, but what was to be

[1] M. Rebelliau, in his admirable chapter in Vol. VIII, 1, of Lavisse's *Histoire de France*.

done with their property ? It was confiscated and applied to charitable and religious uses. But the relatives of the exiles protested, and their claims could not be ignored. The policy of the government varied and its troubles from this source were many.

But more serious and more difficult was the question of the policy to be pursued towards the " new converts." The letters R.P.R. disappear now from official documents for there was no " So-called Reformed Religion " left, and their place is taken by the letters N.C., which imply either New Converts or New Christians, and the term was used for all the Huguenots who had abjured their old faith. The fiction that these men and women had undergone a change of heart and were happy in the fold to which they had been admitted was soon found to be intenable. They very rarely attended the ceremonies of the Church, and their conduct when they did was not edifying. If they were forced to communion protests were raised against the profanation of the greatest of the sacraments. If no pressure was put upon them they remained outside, critical and hostile. It was known that they continued clandestinely to maintain some form of their old religious services. Many who had lived as nominal adherents of the Catholic Church refused the last sacraments when they died. They remained throughout the century an alien element which the Church was quite unable to assimilate.

Then there were the Huguenots who not even

with their lips had consented to abjure their faith. They were quite definitely protected by the Edict of Revocation itself. Its last clause said that, until it should please God to enlighten them, they might live anywhere, continue their trade, and enjoy their property without being troubled on account of their religion on condition that they abstained from all religious exercises. The King believed they were a negligible quantity. He wrote in January 1686, " Of the eight or nine hundred thousand souls who were infected with heresy there remain now hardly twelve or fifteen hundred." But his ministers and intendants knew better. In many parts of France—especially in Languedoc, in Dauphiné, and in Normandy—the numbers were very considerable and their religious exercises were maintained. What was to be done with them ? The government could not make up its mind. Louvois, who had played a prominent part in the measures against the Huguenots before the withdrawal of the Edict, knew the effectiveness of the dragonnades and still applied this instrument of torture. I do not use the word metaphorically. We are particularly well informed of the means employed by the dragoons in this post-revocation period ; they amount to torture in the strict sense of the word. Where religious meetings were held in " the desert " the troops fired on them if they could find them. Many were killed and of the prisoners the men were sent to the galleys and the women to prison. And here, too, torture is hardly too strong a word for their treatment. Life on the galleys was always so hard that it is difficult to realize how human nature could endure it ; many of the Huguenots were by occupation or age unsuited to hard manual toil and a large proportion of them succumbed within a short time. In 1688 another policy was adopted for the moment, and it was decided actually to banish the obstinate Huguenots. But this policy was not followed. The ministers began to return at the risk of their lives, which they laid down in many cases. France grew poorer and her population diminished ; her rivals and enemies (and nearly all the states of Europe were that) grew stronger and richer.

The King's policy was wavering and inconsistent ; as when the order of banishment and the prohibition to emigrate were both to be found at the same time on the statute book. We must remember that the state in the seventeenth century had not the elaborate machinery for enforcing its will which is possessed by the modern state ; and that means of communication, even after Colbert had done his work, were rudimentary. We are thus able to understand how it was that the Huguenots could survive and assemble in the mountains and the forests for religious purposes, though the numbers at such gatherings were small and the flame of hope was difficult to kindle. They had regarded the winning of the English throne by William of Orange in 1688 as a miraculous intervention on behalf of the long-suffering Huguenots, but when the Peace of Ryswick came in 1697 nothing was done for them. The power of France had been checked, but it was by no means broken ; and Louis XIV would not condescend to allow the allies to speak to him of the treatment of his own subjects. But immediately after the Peace, in 1698, there came some practical alleviation of their lot. A new edict was issued and it was accompanied by instructions to the Crown agents as to how it should be applied. Protestant worship was still rigidly forbidden, but the use of violent methods was discouraged. The whole Church in France was called on to live a more regular and devout life ; the conversion of the Huguenots was anticipated as a part of a general religious revival.

France had only three years of peace and then came the greatest and the most disastrous of all Louis XIV's wars—the War of the Spanish Succession. His policy in the matter seems to me to be much too strongly condemned. The hope of uniting the Latin peoples into one great state appealed with overwhelming force to the King and his advisers, and if it had been successful it is possible that much good might have resulted to southern Europe. But it inevitably provoked the hostility of all the rivals of France, and Europe was engaged for thirteen years in a great struggle for the maintenance of the Balance of Power.

While great campaigns were fought in Germany and Italy and Spain and the Netherlands, a little war broke out in France itself, the war of the Camisards in the Cevennes. The district was then thickly covered with forest ; and, though roads had recently been cut through it, the character of the country remained backward and difficult. The repugnance of the population to the Roman faith and practice was not merely the result of Protestant-ism. It dated back to the Albigenses and the religious fermentation of the thirteenth century, but it had felt a strong affinity to the doctrines of Calvin, and the pressure of a common danger had brought about the blending of the two movements. Nîmes, on the edge of the disturbed district, had been a great centre of Protestantism almost from the beginning.

Here as everywhere the government had used much cruelty in the repression of Huguenot movements. The priest, du Chayla, had been no-torious for his cruelties to his religious opponents. In July 1702 his house was forced, his prisoners released, and he himself was murdered. Then, without prearrangement, plan or leaders, a rising or rather a series of risings broke out, and order was not restored for many years. It was in no way an aristocratic movement ; those who took part in it were for the most part shepherds, farmers, and workmen. Its most successful leader was Cavalier, a baker's assistant twenty years of age. He wrote later in England an account of his ad-ventures which is full of interest for the general picture which it gives of the conditions of the move-ment. There was a basis of mystical exaltation in it ; unlettered peasants spoke with tongues and prophesied rather to the scandal of the more sober leaders of the Church. Everything had to be extemporized, arms and powder, soldiers and discipline, hospitals and provisions. Cavalier does not seem to have had at any time more than 2,000 men under his command. But they knew their country, as the Vendean peasants knew theirs a hundred years later, and they inflicted grave losses on the royal troops. Marshal Montrevel was the first leader of the royal armies, but he gained no decisive success. Marshal Villars—one of the greatest of the soldiers of France in this age that produced so many great—had to be called on for the suppression of the revolt, and many thousands of regular soldiers were put at his disposal. The war, as was inevitable, was one of great ferocity on both sides. Cavalier recounts without disguise the burning of churches and the killing of prisoners, and justifies them as reprisals for the worse things done by the other side. Villars, whom Cavalier calls " a polite, fine gentleman," hated the war, as did his soldiers. He had an interview with Cavalier and promised, if we may believe Cavalier's account, that the Camisards [1] should have freedom of conscience and of worship provided that they did not build churches. Cavalier surrendered and accepted a commission in the French army. He had an interview with Louis XIV himself and pressed the claims of his religious allies upon him. He was subsequently sent to the Swiss frontier and then, suspect-

---

[1] This famous name is derived from the habit of the Huguenot insurgents of putting their shirts over their clothes to distinguish one another in a night attack. It had been employed fifty years earlier at the siege of Montauban by Richelieu.

ing foul play, escaped into Switzerland carrying with him all the soldiers he could. He served subsequently with the Dutch and then with the English armies. He was made Governor of the Island of Jersey and was buried in Westminster Abbey. His withdrawal did not bring the war to an end. It smouldered on with many instances of heroism and much cruelty almost to the Peace of Utrecht but we must not follow it farther.

The early years of the century had seen some slackening of the pressure on the Huguenots. But the Great Louis—and there were real elements of greatness in his character—fell during the last years of his life under strong religious influences ; and as a result (it is the greatest tragedy of the story that it was so), his treatment of the Huguenots became more unjust and cruel. Let us take one edict which belongs to the last months of his reign. It is by no means the worst of the cruel series, but it will give us clear and definite proof of the lengths to which the government of France was prepared to go against the heretics. On March 8, 1715, was issued a declaration " in interpretation of that of 29 April 1686." The first document had dealt with the question of relapse. Many men and women who had lived in nominal adhesion to the Catholic Church, when they felt their end draw near, refused to see the curé or to receive the last sacraments of the Church, and sometimes solemnly declared that they wished to die in the R.P.R. The declaration of 1686 had laid down that, if the illness did not prove fatal, the men should be condemned to make public recantation and should then be condemned to the galleys for life and that their property should be confiscated, while the women should have their property confiscated and be imprisoned for life. (And we know what prison meant in the terrible tower of Aigues Mortes and have said something of the living death of the galleys.) If the recalcitrant Huguenots died their property was to be confiscated and their bodies dragged on a hurdle and cast into the common sewer, sometimes with loathsome indignities. These orders had been largely neglected ; partly because the officials were often more merciful than the laws ; partly because it was difficult to be sure whether such obstinate recusants ever had abjured their heresy or whether they were Huguenots living under the protection of the last clause of the Revocation Edict. The new declaration removed that difficulty. In effect—though not in name—it revoked that last clause that had caused so much inconvenience. " We say, declare and ordain, we wish and decide, that all our subjects who are children of parents of the R.P.R., whether born before or after the Revocation of the Edict, who refuse in their illness to receive the sacraments of the church shall be regarded as relapsed and shall therefore be liable to the penalties laid down in the declaration of 29 April 1686." And this monstrous decision is justified on the ground that residence in France since Protestantism has been abolished is a " more than sufficient proof " that they have accepted the Catholic, Apostolic and

Roman religion. But the last clause of the Edict of Revocation still stood on the registers of the Parlement of Paris.

The strongest and best-organized government in Europe had determined that French Protestantism should cease to be. But before the King's death it had given sign of life in a way that was a direct challenge to the royal will. The scattered bones of French Protestantism had drawn together again ; the breath of organic life had breathed through them again ; the hated and terrifying words " synods, colloquies and consistories " were heard once more. This was chiefly the work of Antoine Court. He had seen as a young man something of the struggle in the Cevennes and had been impressed with the need of giving guidance and discipline to the heroic spirits who fought there. On August 21, 1715, eleven days before the death of Louis, he held a synod in the Cevennes, and it was the first of a long series that has not ceased. Soon a training school for ministers was established in Switzerland. Order, discipline and something of the spirit of Calvin returned to the scattered congregations of France. Is there a more remarkable instance of the triumph of faith in history ?

The death of Louis XIV marks the end of a well-defined period. Henceforth quite different forces dominated French history. Nowhere was the change so noticeable as in thought and religion. The strict piety which had prevailed at Court disappeared. The Jesuits fell into disfavour. Their great rivals, the Jansenists, were supported by Parlement and in society. And, at first almost unnoticed, a new current of thought on matters of religion made itself felt with increasing force during the whole century. A number of writers appeared who championed the claims of humanity in all its aspects ; and especially they denounced the cruelties practised in the name of religion. It is the growing strength of this " intellectual movement " which gave its dominant characteristic to the eighteenth century and which contributed most powerfully to the forces which bore France on to the Revolution of 1789. A number of writers appeared who exercised on the thoughts of men an influence such as has rarely belonged to men of letters ; an influence as great as that of Erasmus and Luther and Calvin in the sixteenth century. Of these the most important in his immediate influence on public opinion was Voltaire. He was born in 1694 and was therefore twenty-one when Louis XIV died. He soon began to pour out his barbed shafts against obscurantism and cruelty, and they did not cease to fall until the Revolution was almost in sight. We have no space to speak of those— some of them more profound thinkers—who co-operated with him. Enough that the banner of reason and humanity was very definitely unfurled and an enthusiastic and constantly increasing force gathered round it. It was critical of the religious beliefs of Jesuits, Jansenists, and Huguenots alike ; and we might have expected that in presence of this new and far more serious danger the Christian churches would have forgotten their own differences or at least would not have laid much stress on them, and would have combined against the common enemy. But nothing of the sort happened. The bitter persecution of the Jansenists still continued ; but that does not concern us. It is important, however, to notice that the Roman Catholic clergy of France did not cease for a moment to demand rigorous measures against the Huguenots. There came to them in the end decisive help from the new intellectual movement, for religious toleration was one of the most prominent things in its programme. But Voltaire and his friends showed less appreciation of the sufferings and the heroism of the Huguenots than we should have expected. They regarded them as stern and sour Puritans— Voltaire says half jokingly that he cannot like men who are the enemies of the theatre—who contributed nothing to the enlightenment which was the one thing that these writers prized.

The government of France at Louis XIV's death was vested in a regency, for Louis XV was a child ; and the Regent was the Duke of Orleans, the nephew of the late King. He was completely opposed to the ideas of his predecessor. He lived a life of loose debauchery and made parade of his irreligion. He died in 1723 ; but, though various influences disputed for the control of the young King, nothing like the regime of Louis XIV ever returned to France. In less than fifty years the Jesuits were expelled from France. At no time was there that close union between church and state which had been so characteristic of the last reign.

It is strange that the French Protestants did not profit more quickly from the new turn in the policy of France. In the sixteenth century they had presented a real difficulty and danger to the French Government. They had been a serious obstacle in the path of Richelieu's policy. Behind all the meannesses and cruelties of the action of Louis XIV there had been a genuine religious idealism. But the government of Louis XV carried on a tradition in which it had ceased to believe.

In 1724 there appeared the last of the great laws which regulated the position of the Protestants of France. It was the work of the Bishop of Nantes (de Tressan) who had been associated with the licence of the Regency. He had proposed that some such regulation should be made during the regency of Orleans, but had failed to secure its acceptance. It was after the death of Orleans that the Duke of Bourbon, the chief minister of the young King, agreed to the proposals. It deserves careful examination. No earlier edicts or declarations were withdrawn by it. It was rather a summary of already existing laws with a view to their stricter enforcement. It began with praise of the zeal and piety of the work of Louis XIV and an expression of regret that the enforcement of his laws had of late years grown slack, especially in those provinces which have been " afflicted with the pest." The following is a summary of the provisions.

1. No religious service other than that of the Catholic, Apostolic and Roman Church was to be allowed on pain of the galleys for life and confiscation of property for men who attended. The women were to have their heads shaved and to be imprisoned for life.

2. Death for all preachers ; and the penalty was to be strictly enforced. The galleys for life or perpetual imprisonment for all who assist the preachers, or who do not denounce them.

3. Children were to be baptized in the parish churches within twenty-four hours of their birth. Midwives must give information to the curés of the birth of children.

4, 5, 6, and 7 regulated the education of children of those who are or have been members of the R.P.R. (The abduction of children in order that they might be educated in convents or elsewhere was one of the heaviest trials of Protestant parents.)

8, 9, 10, and 11 dealt with the ugly question of the enforcement of the last sacraments on unwilling Huguenots. We have already noted the nature of the penalties incurred by those who refused the ministrations of the curé in their last illness. But a change for the worse was introduced now, inasmuch as no further evidence was required beyond the statement of the curé, whose offers had been repulsed.

12, 13, and 14 required a certificate from a curé or vicaire that a man was " of good life and character and that he has actually attended the services of the Catholic Church " before he could be admitted to any legal or administrative post ; to any degree in law or medicine ; to occupation as doctor, surgeon, or apothecary ; or to the trade of printer or bookseller.

15. Marriages must be solemnized with the rites of the Church. No other marriages would be regarded as legitimate. Children born of un-recognized marriages would incur the stigma and legal disabilities of illegitimacy.

16, 17, and 18 forbade parents to send their children out of the country to be educated.

In this document—the last that we shall have to analyse—it is noteworthy that there is a constant confusion between those who still make profession of Protestantism under the protection of the Edict of Revocation and those who have accepted Catholicism though their conversion is of doubtful genuineness. The government almost (but not quite), refused to recognize the existence of any avowed Protestants. They must have lived the life of outcasts, excluded from all professions and from the organized trades, or exercising them only with the connivance of their neighbours. Probably in practice their life was rather more tolerable than the letter of the law suggests.

In spite of all, Protestantism still made headway. The edict of 1724 was not more carefully executed than the preceding ones. Huguenot worship was maintained " in the Desert "—that is in secret places, for no churches could of course be built. The organization of the Church was maintained and completed. There had been for some time consistories and local synods. In August 1744 a national synod was held in a remote part of Lower Languedoc and was attended by ministers from all parts of France. The challenge to the government was direct and unmistakable. Even Henry IV and Richelieu had been nervous at the mention of national synods. Now the gathering was all the more alarming because France was at war again with a coalition which included the great Protestant powers of Europe ; and though the assembly prayed " for the preservation of the person of his sacred majesty, for the success of his arms, for the ending of the war, and for the deliverance of the church " the government was not satisfied. A new period of persecution opened with the usual features ; men sent to the galleys for having attended religious services or even for not having denounced them ; children torn from their parents and shut up in convents ; a new emigration into Protestant countries ; heavy financial penalties for the districts where Protestant activity was discovered : and from time to time the brutal execution of preachers. I have throughout shrunk from giving details of the cruelties practised against the Huguenots, but it would not be fair to leave unmentioned the martyrdoms, which were doubtless the seed of their Church as they have been of others. Instead of giving a list of names let me give one or two instances, drawing the account from quite contemporary narratives.

A few lines must be given to the sufferings of the galley slaves, and the heroism with which they were borne. I take the instance from a narrative written by the sufferer himself. Élie Neau had fled from the country in 1679 and had become an English citizen. In 1693 he was taken by a French privateer and brought to Saint-Malo. He was threatened with the galleys if he did not change his religion ; but he refused. " It was on the 3rd of April 1693 that I was tied to the Great Chain with fifty-nine other slaves. It rained almost all that month so that we could hardly travel five leagues a day ; and when we arrived at night at any village they put us, as so many beasts, into stables, where, though always wet and dirty, we often wanted straw to lie upon." When they arrived at Marseilles the chain had grown to 150. " It is indeed a horrid spectacle to see such a number of men fastened to a chain, and exposed to so many miseries that Death is not so hard by half as this punishment." Arrived at Marseilles he was sent on the galley *Magnanime* and was treated with extra severity because he persisted in his faith. Of his sufferings on his galley and in prison it is impossible to write. He always maintained his faith and encouraged his fellow-prisoners to persist in theirs. With the coming of the Peace of Ryswick he was released through the good offices of the British Ambassador to France. He ends his short and very moving narrative by ejaculations of praise and thanksgiving. " Return unto thy rest, O my soul, for the Lord hath dealt bountifully with thee." His sufferings were the common lot of all galley slaves and prisoners in that age ; his

fortitude must be put down to the credit of his
faith.

Jacques Roger had with Antoine Court played
a leading part in the reorganization of the Protestant
Church in France and he had ordained many or
most of the new pastors of the Church. He had
travelled and preached for many years in France,
and the loyalty of his flock and the carelessness or
wisdom of the officials of government had left him
free from serious molestation. He was accused
now of having circulated a false edict purporting
to be a grant of religious toleration, and this may
have been the cause of his arrest. When the agents
of the government came he made no attempt at
flight or concealment. He was seventy years of
age and had no desire to avoid martyrdom. His
condemnation was inevitable, for he had clearly
done many things which the law punished with
death. When his executioners arrived he cried,
" Here then is the happy day that I have so often
desired. Rejoice, my soul, for it is the happy day
on which thou art to enter on the joy of thy Lord."
He recited on his way to the scaffold the psalm
which prays, " O be favourable and gracious unto
Zion ; build thou the walls of Jerusalem." No
torture was applied to him, but he was hanged ;
and, when his body had hung for a day, it was
thrown into the river.

This was in 1745. Our next instance is seventeen
years later, though it would be easy to find others
during the intervening years. François Rochette
had ministered to the Huguenot congregations in

NEW BIRTH OF FRENCH PROTESTANTISM

the Agenois and in Quercy ; it is said that at the time of his death he had twenty-five congregations in his charge. In 1762 he was proposing to go to Saint-Antonin to take the waters there, but on his arrival at Caussade he was requested to turn aside for a baptism. He had to procure guides, and he and his guides were arrested as highway robbers, for there had been much trouble with them in the district. Rochette at once admitted that he was a minister of the Reformed Church, and there seemed no reason to anticipate the worst consequences. However, a strange panic broke out in Caussade. It was reported that the Huguenots were taking up arms to deliver their pastor and his companions, and the population were in fear of a quite imaginary enemy. Three brothers of the name of Grenier who came to Caussade to do what they could for their pastor were arrested. In all, eleven men, including Pastor Rochette, were imprisoned. The case was tried at first in Caussade itself, but was then transferred on appeal to the Parlement of Toulouse ; no ecclesiastical tribunal intervened in any of these cases. In the Parlement a mood of intense hatred of the Huguenots prevailed ; the lawyers were more determined at this juncture to punish heresy than the clergy. All appeals for mercy failed. The pastor's life was undoubtedly forfeit according to the laws, but it is difficult to see how any case could be made out against his companions. On February 18, 1762, the verdict was given. François Rochette was found guilty of " having exercised the functions of minister of the

R.P.R. and of having preached, baptized, administered the communion, and solemnized marriages in assemblies which are known by the name of the Desert." Wherefore he is condemned to be carried with bare head and feet, with a rope round his neck, and placards in front and behind saying, " Minister of the R.P.R.," to the principal door of the church of Saint Stephen. There Rochette shall be made to come down and kneel with a candle of yellow wax in his hands of two pounds weight, and there he shall make amends and ask pardon of God, of the King, and of the ministers of justice for his crimes and misdeeds. Then he shall be taken to the little square of Salin and hanged upon the gallows. All which was exactly carried out, except that the Pastor could not be induced to make amends in the terms prescribed. " I ask pardon of God for all my sins and I believe firmly that I shall be cleansed from them by the blood of Christ who has redeemed us at a great cost. There is nothing for which I need to ask the King's pardon. I have always honoured him as the anointed of the Lord and loved him as the father of his country " ; with much more to the same effect. On arrival at the scaffold he sang the verse of the psalm : " This is the day that the Lord has made ; let us rejoice and be glad in it." Then the executioner did his work. (February 19, 1762.)

Toulouse and its Parlement had acquired a very bad name for cruelty and bigotry. It seems true, though it is hardly credible, that the anniversary of the Massacre of Saint Bartholomew's Day was celebrated annually there with civic and religious processions and public rejoicing. The execution of Rochette and his companions—shameful travesty of justice though it was—had aroused comparatively little attention. But there came in the same year another incident on which the most powerful searchlight in the world was turned, and which became in consequence an important event in the history of France and in the fortunes of the Huguenots. I speak, of course, of the Calas tragedy. It has been told so often and so well that I need only give it in briefest outline.

The Calas family at Toulouse was Huguenot, living under the protection of the last clause in the Revocation Edict. The father, Jean Calas, was sixty-three years of age and kept a draper's shop. One son had abjured Protestantism and had embraced Catholicism but continued on the best of terms with his family. The eldest son, Marc-Antoine, had wished to become a lawyer but had been rejected, because he could not procure a certificate of Catholicism. He is said to have been morose and hypochondriacal. On October 13, 1761, he committed suicide by hanging himself in his father's house. There is really no doubt about the facts. But a wild excitement fell on Toulouse somewhat like that which we have seen at Caussade when Rochette was arrested. It was asserted, and doubtless believed, that the young man had been murdered by his family because he intended to join the Roman Church. The trial was in the hands of the secular Parlement, but the clergy cannot possibly be acquitted of horrible zeal and constant co-operation in procuring evidence. Calas was arrested, was barbarously and repeatedly tortured and then put to death with further tortures. There is no possibility of refusing to believe these terrible cruelties, though one would wish to do so.

Horrible as the story is there must have been many thousands such in the history of Europe, and there was no reason to anticipate that France would grow excited about this; the death of Rochette and his friends had raised no emotion. But the case was brought to the notice of Voltaire in his retirement at Ferney by the Lake of Geneva. He inclined at first to think that Calas was guilty, and he had no special liking for the Huguenots. But when he had convinced himself of his innocence he championed with noble seal the cause of the surviving relatives. His reputation was so great that his voice at once commanded attention; and clearly there was a great volume of humanitarian feeling in France ready to welcome anyone who would attack the cruelty of the law courts. The case was brought before the royal council; the judgment of the Parlement of Toulouse was reversed; Calas was declared innocent by a unanimous vote; some financial compensation was given to the widow. Can any such instance of the vindication of justice by the efforts of a private individual be found in the preceding centuries? Can any other such instance be found until we come to Zola's championship of Dreyfus?

The Rochette and Calas tragedies and others of a similar character must not mislead us as to the character of the age. It was turning rapidly away from the idea of coercion in matters of religion. The Huguenots, in spite of the statutes, were enjoying a far greater liberty than they had done since the Revocation. Protestant meeting-places were being constructed—if we may not yet speak of them as churches. The new spirit of humanity had adherents among the clergy as well as among the men of letters and the laity. The formal attack on the Jesuits in France began in the very year of the execution of Calas. They had already been suppressed, often with great injustice and cruelty, in Portugal and Spain. In 1764 the order was formally abolished by Pope Clement XIII. The appeal of Voltaire on behalf of Calas had found a ready hearing in the royal circle. It is difficult therefore to understand the brutality of the Parlement of Toulouse, and to a less extent of others of the French Parlements. It was not entirely religious fanaticism which inspired them, for the Parlements were foremost in the attack on the Jesuits, and had been the constant champions of the Jansenists. When the Parlement of Toulouse found itself attacked it defended its action not on religious but on political grounds. Heresy, it said, must be suppressed lest it should lead to the overthrow of the state. The Parlements of France were the representatives of the legal class ; they were " the nobility of the gown " and themselves a privileged order. Their action was at least in part the result of professional jealousy and *esprit de corps*.

From the year 1763 onwards the chief interest of French history is to see the gathering of the forces which twenty-five years later plunged the country into the Great Revolution. One feature of this time is the breakdown of the machinery of government. The monarchy was in name absolute, but in fact its authority was challenged on all sides. Laws were not deleted from the statute book, but they were not enforced. The character of the government no longer corresponded to the wishes of the people or of the strongest element in it. Nowhere is this more evident than in the history of the French Protestants. The laws denied their existence. For the offence of attendance at a Protestant form of worship men were serving in the galleys, and women were imprisoned for long years in the tower of Constance at Aigues Mortes and elsewhere. The marriage of Huguenots was not legal unless it was celebrated by a priest. Children born of such marriages were illegitimate and had no right to succeed to the property of their parents. And yet Huguenot ministers travelled about the country ; their lives were forfeit to the law, but they were little molested. Large congregations came together by day as well as by night. Governors and intendants, and even some Parlements, refused to inflict the penalties which the law prescribed. In 1765 an intendant wrote : " The fact is that the baptisms and marriages of the Protestants take place only in their own assemblies—in the

Desert as they are called—which they hold at the gates and within the walls of towns, to which they go in troops in the daytime. Rich Protestants are present there. Ministers and preachers no longer conceal themselves, and are public functionaries. All that remains is to build temples, and that has already been done, for they meet in large numbers in barns that have been specially arranged for the purpose." Two years earlier—in 1763, within two years of the martyrdom of Pastor Rochette—a national synod was held " in the Desert " of Lower Languedoc and there were present 112 pastors or men training for the pastorate. Addresses were voted to the King, though every one there was committing a criminal offence which the law punished with death. Nay more ; all this time the Huguenots had at Court a representative, who constantly pressed their complaints and grievances on the attention of the government. This was Count de Gebelin, a strange, eccentric, and yet attractive figure. He was a savant who plunged with vast industry and courage into the almost uncharted sea of Oriental studies. He was one of the first to interest himself in Egyptology, and believed that the hieroglyphics would give the key to many mysteries ; and he believed in one original language from which all others are descended. His studies were too irregulated to produce much result, but they made him acceptable to the learned society of Paris and served him well in his advocacy of the claims of the Huguenots.

The current set strongly towards religious liberty,

usually under the name of religious toleration. The best-known philosophers cared little for the Huguenots and their cause, but they championed the cause of religious liberty in its most general aspects. A good deal of attention, however, was given to the position of the Huguenots both during the last years of Louis XV and the early years of the reign of the well-intentioned Louis XVI. Thus in 1754 Turgot, then a young man of twenty-seven, had published a little work in which he had advocated the complete separation of Church and state and the toleration of Huguenot worship and organization in all its aspects. If there was any danger in their assemblies it was, he said, because they were forbidden. Give them perfect freedom and all danger would disappear. Several other proposals were made of a more tentative kind. The clergy were caught by the new humanitarian spirit. Rabaut, the greatest of the Huguenot pastors of this time, believed that a great " millenary " revolution was at hand and that all religious bodies—even the Jews and the Roman Catholics—would join together. " In this age more than in any other," he wrote, " it is necessary to simplify religion and to free it from all accessories. It will then be approved of by the philosophers and within reach of the people, which can neither remember nor discuss the mass of articles of which it has been composed, the greater part of which are meaningless to them." Remarkable words to come from a Calvinist preacher ! What would Calvin himself have thought of them ?

The current swept irresistibly towards religious liberty. The Jesuits had been exiled. The Parlements soon followed. Their fall was due to a political quarrel with the government, and they had not all been of the temper of the Parlement of Toulouse. Their suppression, though it was only temporary, made a great change easier. It could not come of course without some strong protests, for the tradition of religious unity maintained by force was too strong to be dropped without an effort. It is one of the curiosities of history that Loménie de Brienne, destined to preside over Louis XVI's last efforts to avoid the Revolution, addressed the King on his consecration in these words : " Sire, you will condemn the councils of an unreal peace and the system of a guilty toleration. We beg of you, sire, not to delay to destroy the hopes of the misbelievers that they may have temples and altars in our midst. It is reserved for you to deliver the final blow to Calvinism. Give orders to disperse the schismatic assemblies and exclude the sectaries without any distinction from all public offices." In 1780 the General Assembly of the clergy demanded a return to the " beaux jours de Louis XIV."

But none could bend Louis XIV's bow now ; and it had broken in his strong grasp. In 1776 Necker, a Protestant from Geneva, took control of the finances. France joined in the war of the American colonies against England and grew enthusiastic for everything American, including freedom in matters of religion. In 1787 the King, not yet willing to call to his help the representative body of the States-General, summoned instead a meeting of Notables—prominent Frenchmen in every walk of life, nominated by the Crown. Lafayette, the hero of France in the United States, brought up the question of the Protestants and demanded civil liberties for them. The King's brother, the Comte d'Artois—later to become the reactionary King Charles X—made himself the spokesman of this measure to the King. Thus came the Edict of Toleration of 1787. It is an important but not an inspiring document. Religious unity is still the avowed aim. The Catholic Religion is alone to have public services. But henceforward non-Catholics may live freely in France ; they may exercise a trade or profession ; they may contract a legal marriage before a legal official ; they can bury their dead according to their own rite.

It was lamentably insufficient, but other changes were bound to come. It was welcomed with great enthusiasm by the Huguenots everywhere ; but history can hardly hear their rejoicings. For France was well in the rapids leading to the Revolution. Such great things were happening that the overthrow of the religious policy of Louis XIV faded from men's memories. All other means of saving France from bankruptcy having failed, Louis XVI recalled the Protestant Necker to office and summoned the States-General. With their meeting in May 1789, the Great Revolution began.

The dykes were cut and the flood spread with unexpected rapidity and volume over the whole country. We are not concerned with it except in so far as it affected the fortunes of the Huguenots as a religious body. We must see, however, the establishment of the principle of religious equality.

The early hopes of moderate and chiefly financial reforms under the presidency of a popular monarchy soon faded away and partly at least through the King's own fault. He or his councillors were alarmed at the spirits that they had let loose. Democracy was demanded in a form that had never been approved of by the philosophers, and equality was the master passion of the hour. Religion was not proscribed nor condemned. The representatives of the clergy had contributed powerfully to the victory of the commons in the early days of the Revolution, though their services in that matter have been too little recognized. But neither Catholicism nor Calvinism nor any form of theology had any hold on the spirit of the States-General, which after the capture of the Bastille and the movement of October 1789, which forced the King to leave Versailles and come to reside in Paris, declared that the making of a Constitution was its chief duty and took the title of The Constituent Assembly. It decided to preface this constitution by a statement of the fundamental principles on which all constitutions should rest, and this declaration it called The Rights of Man. After much debate the Declaration was finished in August 1789 and later became the preface to the Constitution of 1791. Its clauses are published " in the presence and under the auspices of the Supreme Being " and the first article declares that " men are born and remain free and equal in their rights." That clause in itself made all religious exclusion and persecution impossible. But religion was handled definitely in the tenth clause. " No one shall be interfered with for his opinions—not even for his religious opinions—provided their manifestation does not trouble the public order established by law." By the side of this must be put a part of the sixth clause. " All citizens being equal in the eyes of the law are equally admissible to all dignities, offices, and public employments according to their capacity and without any other distinction than that of their virtues and talents."

CHAPTER IX

THE history of the Huguenots ends with the French Revolution ; but French Protestantism does not end there by any means ; and it seems well to give, with even more parsimony of detail than has been observed in the rest of the book, the chief features of its development since 1789.

The Protestants had their troubles during the Revolution, though they were never of the old kind. For a moment the enthusiasms of the hour drew Protestants and Catholics together and the novel scene was presented in some districts of the Catholic curé and the Protestant pastor joining to celebrate the successive stages of the Revolution. Later, when during the Terror royalism saw in the sufferings of the people a chance of restoring the monarchy, the standard of " church and throne " was raised, and an appeal was made to the old passions. At Montauban and at Nîmes, places so full of tragic memories for the Huguenots, there were scenes of the old type. The triumph of the Jacobins put an end to all that, and Catholics and Protestants suffered equally from the later hostility to the Christian religion, expressed in the legislation and still more in the administration of the Jacobins. Rabaut-Saint-Etienne, the most prominent of the Protestants during the Revolution, was guillotined in December 1793 as an adherent of the Girondists. There was much in the principles of that party which was bound to appeal to the old Huguenot spirit.

The welcome given to the development of Napoleon's power was due in some measure to the appeasement which he brought to the religious conflicts. The Christian calendar was restored. The experiment of Theophilanthropy disappeared. Above all, Napoleon as First Consul made with the Pope the religious agreement which is known as the Concordat (July 1801). It was good that the ruler of France should be at peace with the Head of the Roman Church ; but there was a possibility of danger in it for the Protestants. The Pope had wished to have Catholicism declared the religion of the state. Napoleon refused and merely declared in the preamble to the Concordat that " the Catholic, Apostolic and Roman religion is the religion of the great majority of Frenchmen." In the first draft of the religious regulations which was made it was proposed that, while full religious liberty and social equality should be accorded to the Protestants, the Catholic clergy should alone receive a salary from the state and be to a large extent controlled by it. But Napoleon believed in the " totalitarian state " and insisted that the Protestant ministers should receive salaries from the state and thus pass to some extent under its influence and control. A new constitution was drawn up and imposed on the Protestants which had little in common, beyond the name, with the ideas of Church government which had been adopted by Calvin. The Protestants of France were divided into groups of 6,000, and each of these groups was placed under the government of a consistory. But the old democratic leaven was entirely removed from these new consistories. They consisted of the pastors and certain prominent laymen chosen by the state. Synods were mentioned, but were never actually brought into existence. The new arrangement was received with jubilation. " It is no longer in the desert and at the peril of our lives that we render to the Creator the homage which is His due. Our pastors are recognized as public functionaries ; they receive a salary from the government. Our predecessors saw the promised land from Mount Nebo ; but we alone have taken possession of it." It was soon found that the control by the state was very real and had its disadvantages. But Napoleon was careful to mark his appreciation for the loyalty and good character of the Protestants.

Then in 1815 Waterloo brought back the Bourbons ; would it bring back the Bourbon ideal of the relation of religion to the state ? Louis XVIII indeed declared in his charter that all religions were to have the same freedom of worship, but the Catholic, Apostolic and Roman religion was declared to be " the religion of the state," and the phrase might have a dangerous meaning. It was interpreted in a sense most hostile to the Protestants in Provence, where religious passions had always been particularly intense. There was a real reign of terror at Nîmes, at Beaucaire and at Uzès. Many lives were lost and the government seemed in no hurry to restore order. The Catholic clergy are acquitted of any share in the incitement of these scenes of violence, which were chiefly political in their aims. When General Lagarde, the agent of the government, had been assassinated the government determined to take resolute action, and the Protestant form of worship was soon restored in Nîmes and the neighbourhood. The outbreak, serious as it had been, was rather the last gust of the revolutionary storm than a return to the Wars of Religion.

There is little that need be said about the history of Protestantism until the Revolution of 1830. The Pastors were maintained in receipt of their salaries, and these were even increased ; for the restored Bourbons were anxious to strengthen the position of the Roman Catholic Church and the large grants made to it were easier to pass through the assembly when they were coupled with an increase in the stipends of Protestant ministers. There were signs that Charles X might have adopted a policy unfair to the Protestants if his reign had continued ; for the law of sacrilege, which raised so much opposition, defended only the Catholic services from insult. But the Revolution of July 1830 sent him into exile, and in establishing the Orleanist family on the throne introduced a government altogether favourable to the Protestants, if only because it was a conscious imitation of English constitutionalism. Catholicism was no longer declared to be the religion of the state, but only that of the majority of Frenchmen. But the new government, though decidedly hostile to the strongly " Romanist " policy of its predecessor, which had been one of the chief causes of its fall, was not willing to establish complete religious equality. It had to walk warily among its many enemies. Protestants were too few and Catholics too many to make it safe to offend the larger group in the interests of the smaller. So it was judged best to let sleeping dogs lie, and the religious organization of France remained what Napoleon's laws had made it in 1802.

As is well known, the monarchy of 1830 lasted only a few years longer than that of 1815. France had yet to pass through three revolutions before she attained to her present settled and conservative condition. In 1848 there came the second republic with Louis Napoleon as its President. In 1852, President Louis Napoleon became the Emperor Napoleon III. He inaugurated in Europe that criticism of the Parliamentary system and that movement towards a concentrated omnicompetent state under a personal ruler which has in our times assumed such formidable proportions. It is of interest to note how Protestantism fared under him. A further advance was made towards religious equality. There was no longer any word of " a national religion " nor even of " the religion of the majority." Catholicism was not so much as mentioned in the "fundamental law." The only way in which any official pre-eminence was given to the Roman Church was by according its representatives precedence over those of the Protestant community at state receptions. There were some who thought that the time had come to separate Church and state and to make all Churches self-governing communities, free from the control of the state, and no longer in receipt of a state subvention. Those were not, however, the ideas of the Emperor Napoleon, any more than they are those of Mussolini and Hitler. Every department of the activity and thought in France must be brought under the direct guidance of the state and must contribute to its stability and strength. In March 1852 a decree was issued by the government regulating the organization of the Protestant community. It was the direct act of the government decided on after only a perfunctory and unofficial consultation with some of the Protestant leaders. It was maintained that as neither dogma nor worship was touched, the government was not exceeding its proper sphere.

By this "decree of March" something like a parochial organization was given to the Protestant Church of France and in each parochial division a council (*conseil presbytéral*) was set up. The consistory still remained the chief administrative agency of the Church, but its character was much changed. It was to consist henceforth of the members of the parish councils, of all the pastors of the district embraced by the consistory and in addition of laymen from the different parishes. The appointment of pastors was in the hands of the consistory. The most important and interesting change remains to be noticed. The organization of the Protestant Church since 1802 had been exclusive and even plutocratic in character. Only those possessed of a certain property could exercise authority in the Church, and they had formed in practice a close circle, filling up all vacancies by co-option and usually hostile to change. Now Napoleon III was a genuine democrat after a certain fashion. Through all the many changes of his extraordinary career he remained faithful to the idea of " votes for all "—for all men of course —and he believed that order and authority could be founded on this basis. These ideas were now applied to the religious organization of the Protestants. Two years' residence and proved membership of the Church gave any one a right to the vote. The new arrangement introduced a more liberal spirit into the councils of the Church.

Lastly Napoleon instituted a " central council " for all matters concerning the Protestant Churches. It was in form a little like those general synods which had played so great a part in the history of the sixteenth century ; but its spirit and constitution were very different. It consisted of nominees of the government and its vague duty was to co-operate with the government in all that concerned the life of the Protestant Church.

In 1859 French Protestantism celebrated its

tercentenary ; for it dated its birth from the first national synod held at Blois in 1559. The ceremonies and festivities were very largely attended and there was hardly a dissonant voice raised, while the country rejoiced in the triumph of liberty and humanity in the sphere of religion. The victory was definite and is hardly likely to be challenged again ; though the old spirit of dominance and persecution may occasionally be detected in a new disguise.

In the relation of the Protestants to the state only one further change claims attention, but that is an important one. Ever since the Great Revolution there had been ideas of the separation of Church and state and serious proposals had sometimes been made to realize this aim. But nothing had come of them. That the Churches should be controlled by the state in the interest of the state was an idea deeply imbedded in the minds of most politicians. But at the beginning of the century there came a great change. The Dreyfus *affaire* had shaken France to its depths ; that movement had been interpreted as a conflict between Church and state, and it was asserted that the Catholic Church had exercised a dangerous influence on the action of the state. Prominent radical ministers (Messrs. Combes and Briand, were the most important) decided that the connexion between Church and state which went back to the Concordat of Napoleon and behind that to the Concordat of Francis I and behind that again to the long tradition of the Middle Ages, should be broken, and that Churches should be placed on the same footing as any other associations sanctioned by the state. First the chamber voted by very large majorities the following resolution : " The Republic assures liberty of conscience and guarantees the free exercise of religious worship. The Republic does not recognize, does not pay, and does not support any form of worship. The state establishments of religious worship are suppressed." The law giving effect to these principles was passed on December 9, 1905.

The effect of this decision on the Roman Catholic Church does not concern us. The Protestants made no resistance to its passing, though it deprived their ministers of stipends, and subjected the Protestant Churches to certain legal disabilities. But they gained the full right of self-government, which they had never legally possessed during their three centuries and a half of life in France. Consistories of the old kind, provincial synods, national synods now at last appeared as the recognized machinery of Church government and were adopted by both sections of the Protestant Church in France.

For the Protestants of France were no longer a single and united body. Liberty had loosened the union which persecution and suffering had tightened. During the nineteenth century the Protestant community in France had passed through all the phases of religious thought and speculation which had spread over Europe. There had been in the first part of the century a real evangelical revival to which German pietism and the Moravians and, above all, the methodism of John Wesley had contributed. Separate religious groups had been established of those who accepted these views. At the same time the scientific criticism of the origins and documents of Christianity had found many supporters among the Protestants of France ; the foundation of the Revue de Strasbourg by Edmond Scherer in 1850 was an event of great importance. He had resigned his theological professorship at Geneva as a protest against the literalism of the theology that prevailed there. Already in 1849 a " free church " had been founded under the leadership of Frederic Monod and was supported by the famous writer and preacher Edmond de Pressensé.

There are now in France the following Protestant groups or Churches : (1) The Reformed Church with three faculties of theology at Paris, Montpellier and Strasbourg ; (2) the Lutheran Church whose numbers have been materially increased by the reunion of Alsace to France as a result of the Great War ; (3) the Free Churches ; (4) the Methodist Churches, which have since 1852 an organization of their own ; and (5) the Baptist Churches. The *Annuaire Protestant* of 1933 furnishes us with full information about the organization and activities of all sections of French Protestantism. The comparative size and importance of the different groups may be gathered from the numbers of the pastors and ministers who are attached to each. The pastors and evangelists of the Reformed Churches are close on 600. The Lutherans have

240 pastors of whom 170 are attached to Alsace and Lorraine. The Union of Free Churches has 45 ministers ; the Methodists 27 ; the Baptists 41. The *Annuaire* gives a list of about 750 places where Protestant worship of some kind is celebrated. Many of these places have more than one church and the total number passes 800, and this figure, while it includes the colonial churches, does not take into account the Lutheran Churches of Alsace and Lorraine. The buildings no longer hide themselves from the public gaze and some are of considerable architectural interest, though a Protestant writer declares them on the whole to be " lacking in beauty and unfavourable to contemplation." There is much in their services which recalls the sixteenth century and the Puritan conception of life and worship, but a tendency is noted to modify the liturgy in accordance with the principles of " the primitive Calvinist, the Lutheran and the Anglican, so as to give more place to adoration." It is not usually recognized how valuable an element the Protestant Churches of France contribute to the intellectual, social, and religious life of contemporary France.

In conclusion it will be of interest to extract from the *Annuaire Protestant* certain declarations of principle recently issued by the chief French groups. Thus in 1906 the Reformed Evangelical Churches, after the separation of Church and state, issued the following statement : " At the moment when the Reformed Church of France is taking up again the course of its synods which has been

interrupted for so many years it feels before all
things the necessity of thanking God and testifying
its love for Jesus Christ, its divine chief, who has
sustained and consoled it during all its trials. It
declares through its representatives that it remains
faithful to the principles of Faith and Liberty on
which it has been founded. In common with its
Fathers and its martyrs in the Confession of La
Rochelle, with all the churches of the Reformation
in their different creeds, it proclaims The Sovereign
Authority of the Holy Scriptures in matters of
Faith, and salvation by faith in Jesus Christ the
only Son of God." In 1907 the National Union
of the Reformed Churches of France while accepting with some interesting modifications the theological principles of the foregoing declaration pro-
ceeded to declare joyously and with all their heart
the right and the duty for believers and churches
to practice free enquiry in harmony with the rules
of scientific method and to work for the recon-
ciliation of modern thought with the gospel. They
further declare " the definitely lay and popular
character of religious associations, the fraternal
co-operation of all, both pastors and believers, in
the parish each putting at the service of the others
the gifts that he has received." Again in 1912 the
National Union of the Reformed Churches of
France declared that it existed " outside and above
all parties to be a building open to all the children
of the Reformation in France " ; it declared that
it had been prepared by the work and the sufferings
of all those who had never consented to the division

of the glorious Church of the Huguenots ; and that it would remain open to all Christians who wish to maintain the two time-honoured columns of the Protestant faith—Faith and Liberty, Liberty and Faith.

BIBLIOGRAPHY

THE following books are a selection from the wide literature on the Huguenots which will be useful to students.

1. GENERAL

The history of the Huguenots is treated at considerable length in all the histories of France such as those of Martin, Michelet, Lavallée, and Ranke. Dareste's History deserves a special mention because of its strong Catholic sympathies. The " co-operative " history of France edited by Lavisse has excellent chapters on religious topics. The whole subject is treated by Buckle in his *History of Civilization.*

La France Protestante, by Haag (in many volumes), is a series of biographies of Huguenots down to the nineteenth century, and is of the utmost value.

Félice, *Histoire des Protestants de France depuis l'origine de la Réformation jusqu'au temps présent.*

2. TO THE ISSUE OF THE EDICT OF NANTES

The Memoires of Sully, Brantôme, La Noue, Marguerite de Valois, and the letters of Catherine de Médicis.

The history of the religious wars in the writings of Davila, de Thou, and Agrippa d'Aubigné—all contemporaries of the events they describe.

The legal documents are to be found in Isambert's *Recueil des anciennes lois françaises.*

H. M. Baird, an American Scholar, has written largely on the Huguenots ; *History of the Rise of the Huguenots in France, the Huguenots and Henry of Navarre, Theodore Beza.*

M. Romier has thrown new light on the period by his writings. Note especially *Les origines politiques des guerres de religion, Catherine de Médicis, Catholiques et Huguenots.*

Mariéjol, *Catherine de Médicis* is of great value.

For Henry of Navarre, see P. F. Willert, *Henry of Navarre and the Huguenots of France,* and Nouaillac, *Henri IV raconté par lui même.*

Calvin's *Life*, by T. H. Dyer and by R. N. Carew Hunt. A selection of his letters edited by H. F. Henderson.

3. FROM THE ISSUE TO THE REVOCATION OF THE EDICT

Lavisse's own treatment of the subject in his *Histoire de France* may be specially recommended.

R. Lodge, *Richelieu.* Richelieu's *Memoires* and *Testament Politique.* Much light is thrown on the siege of La Rochelle by S. R. Gardiner's *History of England under the Duke of Buckingham and Charles I.*

For the Revocation the essential books are Pilatte, *Recueil des édits, declarations, etc., rendus pour l'extirpation de la RPR*, etc., and Élie Benoît, *Histoire de l'Edit de Nantes.* See too Claude, *Les plaintes des Protestants cruellement opprimés dans le royaume de France.* Among modern books may be mentioned Puaux et Sabatier *Études sur la Révocarion de l'édit de Nantes* and Rebelliau, *Bossuet, historien du Protestantisme.*

The letters of Madame de Sévigné, and of Madame de Maintenon and the Mémoires of Saint Simon will give much light on the feeling of France. Bossuet's works are of course essential.

4. FROM THE REVOCATION OF THE EDICT OF NANTES

For the Dispersion see the Proceedings of the Huguenot Society of London and Lane Pool's *Huguenots of the Dispersion.*

BIBLIOGRAPHY

The sufferings of the Huguenots in France are given in Charles Coquerel, *Histoire des Eglises du Désert* and in Antoine Court, *Histoire des Camisards*. See also Cavallier, *Memoirs of the wars of the Cevennes* ; Athanase Coquerel, *Les forçats pour la foi* and *Jean Calas et sa famille*.

Voltaire's Letters, and Life by Morley, Tallentyre and Parton.

Coignet, *L'Evolution du Protestantisme français*. Charles Bost, *Histoire des Protestants de France*. The *Annuaire Protestant* for 1933.

INDEX